The John Travolta
Scrapbook

The John Travolta Scrapbook

Rob Edelman and Audrey E. Kupferberg

A Citadel Press Book

Published by Carol Publishing Group

A Citadel Press Book
Published by Carol Publishing Group
Citadel Press is a registered trademark of Carol Communications, Inc.

Editorial, sales and distribution, rights and permissions inquiries should be addressed to
Carol Publishing Group, 120 Enterprise Avenue, Secaucus, N.J. 07094

In Canada: Canadian Manda Group, One Atlantic Avenue, Suite 105, Toronto,
Ontario M6K 3E7

Carol Publishing Group books may be purchased in bulk at special discounts for sales
promotion, fund-raising, or educational purposes. Special editions can be created to
specifications. For details, contact Special Sales Department, 120 Enterprise Avenue,
Secaucus, N.J. 07094.

Designed by Andrew B. Gardner

Manufactured in the United States of America

10 9 8 7 6 5 4 3 2 1

Library of Congress Cataloging-in-Publication Data

Edelman, Rob.
        The John Travolta scrapbook / Rob Edelman, Audrey E. Kupferberg.
            p. cm.
        "A Citadel Press book."
        ISBN 0–8065–1813–8 (pbk.)
        1. Travolta, John, 1954–   . 2. Actors—United States—Biography.
    I. Kupferberg, Audrey, II. Title.
    PN2287.T73E33 1996
    791.43′028′092—dc20
        [B]   96–26769
                                                                                              CIP

For
John Travolta
and all his fans

Contents...

Acknowledgments...

several individuals and organizations deserve heartfelt thanks for their assistance during the preparation of this book. They are Sonia Long and the staff of the Amsterdam Free Library, Amsterdam, New York; the Margaret Herrick Library, Center for Motion Picture Study, Academy of Motion Picture Arts and Sciences; Cathleen Anderson; Karen Bjornland; The Bohman-Fannings; Peg Churchill Wright; Ginny, Dick, and Kate Donnelly-Phillips; Barry Gibb; Dick Ashby and Pat Gulino of Gibb Bros Music; Leonard and Alice Maltin; John McCarty; V. A. Musetto; Ron Simon and Gary Rutkowski of the Museum of Television and Radio; the New York Public Library at Lincoln Center; Mary Liz Manning of *Nick at Nite*; Karen O'Hara; David Pietrusza; Renata Somogyi; State University of New York at Albany Library; Amy L. Unterberger; Gretchen Viehmann; and Dr. Alex and Inge Zimmerman.

A special thanks to our editor, Allan Wilson, and our agent, Andy Zack.

Photo Credits

ABC Motion Pictures, Inc.; ABC-TV; Allied Artists; American International Pictures; Arista Records, Inc.; Bryanston; Castle Rock Entertainment; Charly Records Ltd; Columbia Pictures; Columbia Tri-Star Home Video; DC Comics, Inc.; Embassy Films Associates; Filmways Pictures; The Komack Company; LIVE Home Video; MCA TV; Metro-Goldwyn-Mayer Pictures, Inc.; MDP; Midsong International Records, Inc.; Miramax Films; Orion Pictures Corp.; Paramount Pictures; PolyGram Pictures; PolyGram Records; RCA Records; Rysher Entertainment; RSO Films; RSO Records; Savoy Pictures; Touchstone Pictures; Trans World Entertainment; Tri-Star Pictures; Turner Entertainment Co.; Twentieth Century-Fox Film Corp.; United Artists; Universal City Studios; Universal Pictures; Warner Bros; The Wolper Organization.

Linda R. Chen: 115, 123, 160; Patrick DeMarchelier: 92; Richard Foreman: xxi, 134, 137; Paul Jasmin/VISAGES: 95; Bob Marshak: 132, 136; Zade Rosenthal: 140, 141; Firooz Zahedi: 125.

Introduction:
Down . . . But Not Out

"MILLION-DOLLAR SWEATHOG:

Complete with agent, publicist, manager, financial adviser, secretary and lawyer, Kotter's John Travolta *has become a mini-industry."*

—TV Guide, *January 1, 1977*

"JOHN JOSEPH TRAVOLTA:

A Phenomenon on the Scale of Sinatra, Presley"

—Newark Star-Ledger, *August 20, 1978*

"THE CRASH, THE BURN,
THE RETURN:

Twelve years and thirty pounds after **Saturday Night Fever,** *John Travolta's talking about a comeback."*

—New York Newsday, *September 8, 1989*

"THE REAL COMEBACK KID:

Forget the John Travolta you thought you knew— **Pulp Fiction** *obliterates his light-weight image forever."*

—New York Newsday, *September 18, 1994*

(Opposite) Travolta, in the best shape of his life, reprising Tony Manero in *Staying Alive.*

Travolta as Tony Manero, Karen Lynn Gorney as Stephanie, on the 2001 Odyssey dance floor in *Saturday Night Fever*—one of the most famous and enduring images of late 1970s pop culture.

The essence of the career of John Travolta may be summed up in these newspaper and magazine headlines. The first two reflect his astonishing popularity in the late 1970s, when he graduated from teenybopper's delight on TV to disco-gyrating phenomenon in the movies. The last two hint at his career fadeout in the 1980s, and his subsequent mid-1990s resurrection as a world-class star.

In 1977 and 1978, the dimpled, six-foot-tall actor with the broad smile, slick dark hair, and baby-blue eyes—described by gossip columnist Liz Smith as "the most startlingly beautiful since Elizabeth Taylor's" —was the hottest thing in movies. He had won his initial fame as Vinnie Barbarino, Sweathog supreme, on television's *Welcome Back, Kotter*. Adolescent girls swooned over him, and he became a much-adored sex symbol, a more youthful version of his good friend Sylvester Stallone's Italian Stallion. Next, Travolta was propelled to big-screen superstardom in *Saturday Night Fever* as Tony Manero, Brooklyn paint store clerk by day and disco dreamboat by night. His follow-up was the even more popular *Grease*, the screen version of the long-running Broadway musical ode to an idealized 1950s.

Travolta's painless transformation from television celebrity to major movie star was evidence that he would not suffer the professional decline of countless TV-created pop culture heroes. Like Bobby Sherman and Shaun and David Cassidy, he had become an icon for adolescent girls, but Sherman and the Cassidys were unable to sustain their careers.

Not all of Travolta's early admirers were teenagers. A tuxedoed young superstar is pictured signing autographs for some of his older fans.

Kotter colleagues Ron Palillo, Lawrence-Hilton Jacobs, and Robert Hegyes, each a talented actor, could not regain the popularity they enjoyed as Travolta's fellow Sweathogs. As one year eases into the next, endless numbers of young actors are announced as "the new James Dean," only to become flavors-of-the-month (if not the week or day). One such celebrity-as-flickering-light is Edd "Kookie" Byrnes, who in the late 1950s became the rage as the jive-talking parking lot attendant on *77 Sunset Strip*. Two decades later, when he made a cameo appearance in *Grease*, his presence was little more than a nod to 1950s nostalgia.

Personalities like Byrnes enjoy a vogue for a few years, only to watch their popularity disintegrate. Would this be the case with Travolta? Would his core group of fans tire of him once they grew beyond their teens?

Not to the way of thinking of Pauline Kael, that most influential of film critics. Kael captured the essence of Travolta's charisma, which very well might have allowed him to segue from *Welcome Back, Kotter* and *Saturday Night Fever* and *Grease* into a stellar movie career. Of his performance in Brian DePalma's *Blow Out*, Kael observed, "Playing an adult [his first], and an intelligent one, Travolta has a vibrating physical sensitivity like that of the very young Brando . . ." She compared his ability to expose his emotions on screen to that of Brando in *On the Waterfront*.

Travolta already had been contrasted to other screen icons. "In the timeless manner of movie sex symbols," noted Frank Rich in his *Time* magazine review of *Saturday Night Fever*, "his carnal presence can make even a safe Hollywood package seem like dangerous goods." *US* magazine reported in 1978 that "... critics now mention him in the same breath as Brando and Pacino," and Roger Ebert observed that "Travolta is a phenomenon on the scale of Sinatra, Elvis, or James Dean."

On April 3, 1978, Travolta made the cover of *Time* magazine. He was pictured in a disco-dancing pose, with his hips rotating as if his body were freeze-framed in the middle of a swirling Hula Hoop motion. The headline TRAVOLTA FEVER was plastered across his waist. The feature story inside compared Travolta's presence in *Saturday Night Fever* to the star-making turns of Robert De Niro in *Mean Streets*, Al Pacino in *The Godfather*, and Dustin Hoffman in *The Graduate*. "Of course, this is heady company to be keeping," noted *Time*, "and plunging a twenty-four-year-old with little formal acting training into its midst is probably unfair. Yet suddenly, with one movie, Travolta can be mentioned in that league without apology."

The kudos kept on coming—for a while, anyway. "He's a combination of Monty Clift and Clark Gable," remarked Robert Evans, coproducer of Travolta's *Urban Cowboy*, released in 1980. "He reminds me so much of Monty Clift," added the film's director, James Bridges. That same year, *Time* magazine noted, "Many observers have compared [Travolta's] presence—volatile and vulnerable—to Montgomery Clift's; his rebellious edge and androgynous appeal have prompted comparisons with Brando and James Dean. But it is in his raw, narcissistic sexuality— a sexuality so intimate and exposed it's almost embarrassing to look at— that he evokes the first great male sex object of the movies, Valentino."

In 1978, *Rolling Stone* pronounced that Travolta would be "revered forever in the manner of Elvis, James Dean, [and] Marilyn Monroe." However, what all these pundits were forgetting was that, in the lexicon of American pop culture, nothing is forever. You are only as good as your last movie. The three cited stars all died young, thus mythicizing their legends. Travolta was very much alive, and still had a great deal to prove as a performer.

That same year, Lorne Michaels, producer of *Saturday Night Live*, remarked that Travolta "is the perfect star for the seventies. He has this strange androgynous quality, this all-pervasive sexuality. Men don't find him terribly threatening. And women, well . . ." That formula may have fit the 1970s. But what of the next decade?

As it turned out, by the late-1980s Travolta's name had been stricken from the movie personality A-list. He believed that this decline resulted from his having been dislodged by a group of newer stars. "Up until 1985, I think I made all the choices I was supposed to make," Travolta recalled in 1994. "But when the onslaught of wonderful young actors came on the scene—Tom Hanks, [Tom] Cruise, [Kevin] Costner, Mel Gibson—it was suddenly less interesting to give me all the best scripts. It wasn't that there weren't hits, or some good work after that, but it wasn't at the top level. I had to settle for third and fourth choices and make the best of what was offered to me."

Because he had attained superstardom at such a young age, it may have seemed that Travolta was the senior of the actors he cited. But three of the four are virtually the same age; he is just a year older than Costner, and two years the senior of Gibson and Hanks. The reality of his situation was that, even when he still was considered a top-flight star, Travolta was

Travolta as Danny Zuko and Olivia Newton-John as Sandy in *Grease*.

unable to sustain his status with a role as stunning as that of Tony Manero.

In the late 1970s, Travolta had been a trendsetter. But disco and polyester suits, like Hoola Hoops and the twist before them, were fads embraced by an ever-fickle public—and *Saturday Night Fever* had inexorably linked Travolta with disco and polyester suits. Those who chanted "Disco is dead," a refrain of the early 1980s, also were, in essence, declaring: "Polyester is dead." "The hustle is dead." "Donna Summer's music is dead." "John Travolta's career is dead."

In 1983, Travolta reported that Warren Beatty had offered him some sage advice: "You have two of the biggest movies in movie history. Why do you need another one? Just do good movies, John." But Travolta was having a difficult time heeding Beatty's counsel. *Urban Cowboy*, in which Travolta attempted to do for country western chic what *Saturday Night Fever* did for discothèques, was far from a failure. But neither did it pump up his career. Pauline Kael's comments aside, *Blow Out* was not a very good film, and it was a box-office disappointment. *Staying Alive*, in which he reprised the role of Tony Manero, made money, but it was lambasted by critics and added little to his resume. *Two of a Kind* and *Perfect*, his final major releases of the mid-1980s, were ill-conceived, and became out-and-out career-killers.

Travolta's appearance in *Look Who's Talking*, a sleeper hit comedy released in 1989, was considered an aberration. His filmography was becoming littered with the likes of *Shout, Eyes of an Angel, Chains of Gold* . . .

Prior to his "has-been" years, Travolta had been marketed to the public in four different stages. In his *Welcome Back, Kotter* days, he was sold as a teenybopper dreamboat. After the release of *Saturday Night Fever*, he graduated to disco king. After disco died and *Urban Cowboy* came to movie theaters, he stood at the vanguard of country-western chic. Finally, by the time of *Staying Alive*, Tony Manero and the core audience for *Saturday Night Fever* were over twenty-one. So Travolta was re-created one last time via the lowest common denominator of raw, near-naked sex. He was Mr. Stud, a candidate for a *Playgirl* magazine centerfold.

Travolta, as Vincent Vega, and Samuel L. Jackson, as Jules Winnfield: ready to rumble in *Pulp Fiction*. © Miramax Buena Vista.

All of this is epitomized by the manner in which he was depicted in his various *Rolling Stone* magazine cover stories. Since it is no teen fanzine, Travolta-as-Barbarino was not highlighted in the magazine. But his three other personae were. Travolta graced the *Rolling Stone* cover of June 15, 1978, in Tony Manero–like garb: a double-breasted polyester blazer and untucked plaid shirt with long, pointed collar. Writer Tom Burke's feature was headlined "Struttin' His Stuff." Two years later, on July 10, 1980, a completely new Travolta emerged. Here he sported a cowboy hat and western belt and boots, and was shown kicking up his heels western-style. The article, by Timothy White, was titled "True-Grit Tenderfoot." Three years after that, on August 18, 1983, Travolta—minus his body hair and garbed only in a skimpy, jagged-edged loincloth—flexed his muscles on another *Rolling Stone* cover. The feature, written by Nancy Collins, was titled "Sex and the Single Star." Inside were two additional revealing photos of Travolta. One was a *Playboy/ Playgirl*-like centerfold, in which he flashed his smile and wore next to nothing. In the other, he was statuesquely posed; it was cropped at the point where his pubic hair begins, suggesting that he might have been posing in the nude.

Travolta had proven himself to be no Brando, no Pacino, no Elvis.

None of these performers ever had to remove his clothes in a bid to hype a new movie and preserve his popularity.

It was Travolta's good fortune that he did not have to work to pay his rent. He had earned a mint not just from acting in movies but also from the soundtrack albums of his films. He had wisely invested his earnings, and it has been said that he is a millionaire who lives like a billionaire. A vacation for Travolta means not just renting a yacht. The craft must be a "double-o-seven type," with all the accoutrements including helicopter and seaplane. Over the years, he has indulged his hobby of flying by purchasing planes and constructing landing strips on his properties. On a lesser but no less extravagant level, one Christmas he installed trees in all of the bedrooms in his twenty-room home on an island in Maine's Penobscot Bay.

If Travolta wanted to continue acting after his mid-1980s decline, what would have been next for him? A role in a dinner theater production of *The Odd Couple*, costarring with a middle-aged David Cassidy? An Edd Byrnes–like appearance in a *Grease* revival?

What happened next in his career only can be described as astounding. How many has-been actors are able to reinvent themselves, and rise above the purgatory of direct-to-video movies, the way Travolta did in *Pulp Fiction*?

Not many.

A few stars have been able to make over their screen personae as their careers progressed. Dick Powell was one, transforming himself from a pretty-boy ingenue-crooner in 1930s Warner Bros. musicals to hard-bitten hero of 1940s film noirs. In his earliest movies, Elvis Presley was an angry young rocker, but in his post-army career he successfully was desexed. By the 1960s, he was no longer Elvis-the-Pelvis; he had become more hero than antihero as his original fans left their teen years and his on-screen image came to resemble the all-American guy-next-door.

Joan Crawford began in movies during the 1920s as a devil-may-care flapper. During the following decade, she was transformed into a

Travolta in one of his better post-*Saturday Night Fever* roles: Jack, the motion picture soundman, in *Blow Out.*

hardened, Depression-era heroine. After being written off as box-office poison, and having been let go by her studio, MGM, she emerged in the 1940s to win an Oscar as *Mildred Pierce*, and she completed her career resuscitation by playing anguished heroines and femmes fatales. She altered herself one more time, in the 1960s, becoming a fright-film star after being cast opposite Bette Davis in *What Ever Happened to Baby Jane?*

But most performers who start out on top are unable to maintain stardom as successfully as Crawford. If they are fortunate, they reemerge after their days of prominence, when they no longer can rely on their looks or their youth, to become respected supporting and character actors.

It is rare and remarkable for an actor whose A-list status had been ended for over a decade—an eternity in the lexicon of pop culture—to rematerialize as a star, shining with more strength than ever before. Yet Travolta did just that in *Pulp Fiction*, playing hip hit man Vincent Vega and emerging as a mature, tough, supercool dude in the style of Humphrey Bogart, Edward G. Robinson, John Garfield, and his idol, James Cagney. In *Pulp Fiction*, Travolta offers glorious evidence that his talent had been present all along. It just had been misused.

Travolta's career progression most resembles that of Frank Sinatra, star crooner of the 1940s, when he packed in the bobby-soxers at the Paramount Theater on Broadway. By the early 1950s, he was considered a has-been. In *Meet Danny Wilson*, released in 1952, he essentially played himself: a cocky saloon singer who makes it big, and even sings to screaming teenyboppers at the Paramount. The songs Danny croons, beginning with *I've Got a Crush on You* and *She's Funny That Way*, already were Sinatra standards.

The simple fact was that, in *Meet Danny Wilson*, Sinatra's talent was being improperly tapped. While reminding viewers of his past glories, the film is a lightweight vehicle which did nothing to revive his career. Sinatra was to resurrect himself for all time a year later, proving that he could act as brilliantly as he sang, as he won an Oscar for playing Angelo Maggio, the skinny, tough, ill-fated marine in *From Here to Eternity*.

Similarly, at a time when Travolta's career was in decline, the films in which he appeared, in addition to being clinkers, often reminded audiences of his past as a disco icon. Instead, they should have attempted to create a new cinematic image for the actor. But the difference between Travolta and Sinatra is that the latter's career was shut down only for a few years. Travolta's comeback happened after a decade-long hiatus.

When Travolta won an Academy Award nomination for *Saturday Night Fever*, some felt that the citation was gratuitous. Similar to Julia Roberts's nomination for *Pretty Woman*, it was a reward for a promising young actor who had been lucky enough to land a star-making role in an out-of-left-field box-office smash. Even though he had earned fine reviews —David Ansen, writing in *Newsweek*, summed up the critical reaction by dubbing his performance "fresh, funny, downright friendly"—Travolta *was* a newcomer. And after all, wasn't Tony Manero just a variation of Vinnie Barbarino? Travolta may have had talent, but did he have range?

There were no naysayers when the new, improved Travolta—with range to spare—won his second Oscar nod for *Pulp Fiction*. Even more important, *Pulp Fiction* would be no fluke, no one-shot. In his follow-up

(*Opposite*) "Ain't it cool!"—Travolta, with heavier artillery, in *Broken Arrow.*

release, *Get Shorty*, Travolta played another suave but tough gangster, this one a Miami loan shark turned Hollywood producer, giving a performance that was just as lively, just as vivid and memorable. His acting was equally Oscar-worthy, but he did not win a nomination. *Get Shorty*, in fact, was completely shut out of the Oscars, perhaps because Academy voters were not amused by a scenario in which a mobster fits in so easily among their minions.

This disappointment did not in any way diminish the new Travoltamania. In February 1996, around the time the nominations were announced, the actor appeared on *The Tonight Show* to promote his latest film, *Broken Arrow*. In introducing him, host Jay Leno called Travolta "the hottest man in show business." Later that month, he attended the Berlin Film Festival, where *Get Shorty* was screened. *Variety* ran a photo of Travolta accompanying an article on the festival's opening days, headlined STARS LIGHT BERLIN AS MARKET AWAITS SPARK. Reporter Erik Kirschbaum observed that Travolta "attracted blinding attention from scores of photographers and TV crews at the screening."

That same month, Travolta again appeared on the cover of *Rolling Stone*, adorning the issue dated February 26. This time, he was attired in neither polyester blazer, cowboy hat, nor loincloth. None of these accoutrements were necessary. All you saw of the mature Travolta was a close up of his face, his baby blue eyes staring out at you. A headline, printed in large orange letters at the left of his forehead, announced what Travolta had become since his first moments on screen in *Pulp Fiction*: "Mr. Cool."

All Travolta has to do to maintain his popularity well into the next century is choose his roles wisely, appearing in films which fully exploit his talent and charisma. If he succeeds, he will be firmly established as the Humphrey Bogart and James Cagney of the twenty-first century.

And if he *really* succeeds, given the fickleness of popular taste, Bogart and Cagney eventually may be viewed as the Travoltas of their time.

The John Travolta
Scrapbook

One

You Must Have Been a Beautiful Baby

John Joseph Travolta, the baby in a family of six children, was born in Englewood, New Jersey, on February 18, 1954. He entered the world at 2:53 P.M., weighing in at seven pounds, nine ounces. His mother, Helen (née Burke), was a drama teacher, director, and former actress. She once toplined a group known as the Sunshine Sisters, and back in 1931 set a long-distance mark for swimming the Hudson River. Helen Travolta even makes a brief appearance in *Saturday Night Fever*, billed as the "Lady in Paint Store." His father, Salvatore, was an ex-semipro football player and co-owner of the Travolta Tire Exchange in nearby Hillside.

"They really adored each other," Travolta recalled of his parents in 1983. "My father thought my mother was the living end, that she was the best actress, the best director, and had the most style, presence, and personality of anyone he had ever known. They had a very hot relationship. Even after they'd been married twenty-seven years, you could walk into their bedroom in the morning—like I sometimes did as a kid—and there they'd be, nestled in each other's arms, their bodies totally locked together. They were really into each other."

Throughout his life, Travolta has remained close to his family. His childhood was a happy one, in which both of his parents made him feel secure and loved. His mother gave him unadulterated affection, while he and his father would pass hours together working on projects around the house. In fact, during a 1995 interview, he explained that the expensive cigar he was nursing reminded him of his father.

Travolta grew up in the same frame house in which his parents continued to reside after his *Kotter/Fever* success. His siblings are Ellen, Sam, Margaret, Ann, and Joey, respectively fifteen, ten, seven, five, and three years his senior. In 1978, just as he was enjoying his first dip into celluloid superstardom, he noted, "I could always express my feelings to [my family], and they could say almost anything to me. The love was there and still is." Eight years later, he reminisced, "We were a theatrical family.

(Opposite) Travolta as Vinnie Barbarino from *Welcome Back, Kotter.*

My mother loved [the Golden Age of Hollywood]. We have pictures of her holding my sister Ellen up and kissing her in profile like the stars did in magazines."

At his birth, both of Travolta's parents were in their forties. "I'm realizing that for so much of my life I had an older viewpoint; I saw things as an older person," he remarked in 1985. "That's common among change-of-life babies. So I have this dichotomy where I'm either like super young or I feel like I'm coming to the end of my years."

All of Travolta's siblings became involved in show business. In fact, the actress who appeared as Mrs. O'Hara, Sweathog Arnold Horshack's mother on *Welcome Back, Kotter*, was sister Ellen Travolta. She also acted with her brother in a summer theater production of *Bus Stop*. Her other credits include the Broadway production of *Pajama Game*, *Irma La Douce*, and *The Mad Show*; the Broadway and touring productions of *Gypsy*, starring Ethel Merman; and the TV series *Makin' It*, *Number 96*, *Joanie Loves Chachi*, and *Charles in Charge*. In the last two, she appeared as Scott Baio's mother. "I consider myself a substantial working actress," Ellen once observed. "I'm not a star, and I'm not a sex symbol. God, no! I'm a character woman."

In the wake of *Saturday Night Fever*, Travolta's brother Joey was placed on the Paramount Pictures payroll at $50,000-a-year. His shot at fame came as the star of the 1979 movie *Sunnyside*, in which he attempted to do for the New York borough of Queens what John already had done for Brooklyn. Joey T. played Nick Martin, a nice-guy street kid with a gang-member past who wants to take on the rival Savage Warlocks before moving on to Manhattan. The critics—and, more important, the public— were less than kind to *Sunnyside*. The *Variety* scribe noted, "John Travolta's brother Joey is okay in his pic debut, but the role's so bland and the film's so bad that lightning won't strike twice, at least this time out." Joey was to have no second chance at stardom. Instead, he appeared on television series and in such films as *Amazon Women on the Moon* (a parody film which also featured John's wife-to-be, Kelly Preston), *Hollywood Vice Squad*, *Hunter's Blood*, *The Prodigal*, *Round Trip to Heaven*, *They Still Call Me*

After Travolta won big-screen fame in *Saturday Night Fever*, his older brother, Joey (*above, center*), had a shot at cinema stardom in *Sunnyside.*

Bruce, and *3 Ninjas Kick Back*. In the 1990s, he began directing movies; in 1996, he went into preproduction on *Navajo Blues*, starring Steven Bauer.

Sister Ann Travolta played Rizzo in the national company of *Grease*, and appeared in productions of *Zorba*, *George M*, and *Hello, Dolly!*. She acted onstage with her brother in the summer theater production of *Bus Stop*, and has small roles in four of John's films: *Saturday Night Fever* (billed as Pizza Girl), *Urban Cowboy* (as a member of a wedding party), *Two of a Kind* (as a bank teller), and *Perfect* (in the role of Mary). Brother Sam Travolta also appears on-screen in *Perfect*, as a hotel desk clerk.

As a youngster, Travolta showed an interest in the theater. In a 1978 interview, his mother observed, "He was a lonely child. All the others were grown up or at school. I took him to watch rehearsals at my high school drama class and he was glued."

He became enamored of *Gypsy*, and spent one summer with sister Ellen when she was touring with the musical. He went about memorizing the entire show and all of the roles, the women's as well as men's, and then would put on performances for his parents.

Travolta took dancing lessons with Gene Kelly's brother, Fred, and at twelve, he enrolled in a local acting workshop sponsored by the Actors Studio, and won a role in a production of Frank D. Gilroy's *Who'll Save the Plowboy?* He also performed in summer stock and dinner theater, most notably in *Gypsy* and *Bye, Bye Birdie*. And at sixteen, he quit Dwight Morrow High School in Englewood to pursue a career as an actor. "I was anxious to get my life going, because I was bored and trapped at school," he once noted. "I knew what I wanted."

Travolta's siblings, on occasion, have had small roles in his films. Such was the case in *Perfect*, which featured Sam Travolta (*Opposite above* with brother John) as a hotel desk clerk and Ann Travolta (*Opposite below* with Jann Wenner) as a *Rolling Stone* assistant.

His mother was amenable to his quitting school. But his father made him promise to return in one year if his career did not progress. Needless to say, Travolta never did complete high school.

He moved to Manhattan, where he first bunked in the apartment of a sister and later moved into a coldwater flat. He soon had picked up a pair of agents, Bob LeMond and Lois Zetter. LeMond initially had seen him in the production of *Bye Bye Birdie*, in which he played Hugo Peabody—and earned $50 a week. "I was dragged out there [by a friend] yelling and complaining," LeMond recalled. "Well . . . I couldn't take my eyes off of him. I went backstage to congratulate him and suggested he give me a call."

LeMond and Zetter would play meaningful roles in the establishment of Travolta's career. The actor remained with them until 1982, at which point he signed with Michael Ovitz at the Creative Artists Agency. Three years later, he left Ovitz, and has since been managed by Jonathan D. Krane, the producer of several of his films.

Back in 1972, all of this was in Travolta's future. In March of that year, when he had just celebrated his eighteenth birthday, he was cast in an Off-Broadway revival of John Colton and Clemence Randolph's *Rain*, playing the role of Private Griggs. The show's cast list began with Madeleine Le Roux, James Cahill, Beeson Carroll, Elizabeth Farley, Paul Milikin, Patricia O'Connell, Bernie Passeltiner, Antonia Rey, Richard Ryder, and Ben Slack, and ended with John Travolta. *Rain* closed after five performances.

But Travolta's career was beginning to roll. Between 1972 and 1974, he appeared in guest roles on the television series *Owen Marshall, Counsellor at Law* (airing December 14, 1972), *The Rookies* (October 1, 1973), and *Medical Center* (December 16, 1974). For nine months, beginning in December 1972, he played the role of Doody in the original national touring company of *Grease*. One of the fallacies relating to Travolta's career is that he was in the show's original New York cast. Not so. James Canning played Doody, while Barry Bostwick starred as Danny Zuko. Prior to his appearing in the screen version, Travolta's major *Grease* connection was playing Doody on tour; he then made his Broadway debut in the role. In December 1979, he and sister Ellen were in the audience at the Royale Theater for performance number 3,243 of the musical: a milestone which made *Grease* the longest running show in Broadway history to that time, surpassing *Fiddler on the Roof*. In February 1992, Travolta and his wife, Kelly Preston, attended a *Grease* "20th Anniversary Class Reunion" celebration at the Sheraton Universal Hotel in Los Angeles.

In 1974, Travolta won a supporting role in *Over Here!*, a Broadway musical starring the surviving Andrews Sisters, Patty and Maxene. If *Grease* was 1950s nostalgia, *Over Here!* was an ode to the pop culture of the 1940s personified by the Andrews Sisters. Travolta's part was small: his character was named Misfit, and he was one of a group of singing and dancing soldiers heading off to battle. His *Playbill* mini-biography noted that he was "born into a theatrical family"; "had recently appeared on TV's *The Rookies*"; had roles on "the daytime series *Edge of Night* and *The Secret Storm*"; "made his Broadway debut as Doody in *Grease*, a role he created in the first National Company"; and "made his stage debut as Bobby in *The Boy Friend* at the Allenberry Playhouse."

Of course, Patty and Maxene were cited in the reviews, as were Janie Sell, Ann Reinking, Samuel E. Wright, John Mineo, and other performers. You would be hard-pressed to find any extended mention of Travolta. However, John Beaufort, critiquing the show in the *Christian Science Monitor*, did list several "numbers circled on my program," one of which was " 'Dream Drummin'/Soft Music' [with John Travolta leading the band, all in gold dinner jackets]."

At that time, the name of the unknown young actor was proving to be too unwieldy to spell. In the indexes of the *New York Times Theater Reviews*, the misspellings were "Travotta" in the listing for *Rain* and "Travoita" in the citation for *Over Here!*. In an earlier, pre-Pacino/De Niro era, perhaps Travolta would have had his name changed, eliminating all ethnic connotation. He might have been rechristened with a rock-solid, all-American sounding appellation, as had been entertainers as diverse as Dino Crocetti (who became Dean Martin), Concetta Rosalie Ann Ingola

(Connie Stevens), Robert Walden Cassotto (Bobby Darin), Anthony Benedetto (Tony Bennett), and Anna Marie Louise Italiano (Anne Bancroft).

But *Over Here! was* Broadway, and it *was* another impressive credit on the résumé of a young actor just past his twentieth birthday. The show debuted at the Shubert Theater in March 1974, and went on to run for 348 performances. This was not to be Travolta's final appearance onstage. During the summer of 1976, after he had become a teen fave on *Welcome Back, Kotter*, he starred while on hiatus from the show as Bo Decker in a New England summer theater production of William Inge's *Bus Stop*, costarring Anita Gillette. One of the production's venues was the Falmouth Playhouse on Cape Cod. Prior to its opening, the theater program confirmed Travolta's appearance by announcing, "YES, IT'S TRUE! In two weeks, beginning Monday, July 26 thru Saturday the 31, you will see John Travolta (TV's Barbarino in *Welcome Back, Kotter*) and Anita Gillette in the wonderful William Inge comedy, *Bus Stop*. Reserve your seats now for this one, sure to sell out soon!"

Along with other young actors, Travolta paid his bills partly by doing voice-overs and appearing in television commercials. Reportedly he was seen in over forty ads. A typical one was for Right Guard, in which he and two other clean-cut types are depicted as basketball players who sing the praises of the deodorant while in the locker room.

In 1974, Travolta starred in thirty- and sixty-second versions of a commercial for the Mutual of New York Life Insurance Company. "We saw him first on videotape," recalled Marshall Karp, cocreative director at the Marschalk ad agency, at the time Travolta was riding high in *Saturday Night Fever* and *Grease*. "We knew that the kid was going to be a star." Added Andrew Langer, Karp's partner, "He was excellent. He looked at the camera, delivered his lines, and the hair on the back of your neck stood up." For shooting a test commercial, Travolta was paid $200 for a day-and-a-half of work. He already had moved to California when it came time to shoot the complete ad, so he was flown back to New York. Through 1976, he had earned about $3,800 in residuals from the ad.

Two

A Hot New Sex Symbol

Travolta earned his initial mainstream stardom as Vinnie Barbarino, one of "four uproariously obstreperous misfits" (as described in the *Variety* review of the premiere episode) in the television sitcom *Welcome Back, Kotter*. In a classic understatement, the young actor declared, several months into playing Barbarino, "I remember, at the audition, I said to myself, 'Gee, if I can pull this one off, I'm doing pretty well.'" The show's executive producer, James Komack, recalled, after the show had become a hit, "I had seen five or six guys, but the moment I saw John I knew he was it."

The show premiered on ABC on September 9, 1975. Its premise: Brooklynite Gabriel Kotter (Gabe Kaplan) returns to his old school, James Buchanan High, to be the home room and social studies teacher of the Sweathogs, a bunch of supposed incorrigibles. The two other adult characters on the show were Kotter's wife, Julie (Marcia Strassman), and Arnold Woodman (John Sylvester White), the schools' vice-principal. Prior to its premiere, Komack explained, "I like to think of it as a 1975 *Blackboard Jungle*, or an up-to-date version of the Dead End Kids, but with laughs. We went to New York and picked four naturals to play the main student parts. . . . They're perfect for what we want to show—what goes on in a classroom in a poor section of town."

At the show's outset, Travolta was the leader of this gang of four, his fellow Sweathogs being Juan Luis Pedro Phillipo de Huevos Epstein (Robert Hegyes), Arnold Horshack (Ron Palillo), and Freddie "Boom-Boom" Washington (Lawrence-Hilton Jacobs). The first episode shows Kotter as a newly assigned teacher at Buchanan. He tells Julie that the school is "in Bensonhurst, which is in Brooklyn, which is where I spent four degenerate years as a student." That may have been a decade earlier, but some things at the school have not changed. One is the presence of Woodman, his nemesis, whom Kotter accidentally calls "Woodface." Another is the term *Sweathog*, introduced by Kotter during his own student days.

(Opposite) Barbarino, in an "up your nose with a rubber hose" mood.

Travolta, ever-resplendent as Vinnie Barbarino.

As Kotter enters his classroom, Barbarino is sitting on the teacher's desk. Seeing Kotter, he takes his own seat. He and his fellow Sweathogs respond to Kotter's presence like automatons as the teacher tells his students that he wants to "know who you are." Kotter motions to the Sweathogs on one side of the room to begin introducing themselves. Now comes Barbarino's first words on the show: "No. No. We're gonna start over here," he says, from the other side of the room. He then stands up and smiles mischievously. "Barbarino. Vinnie Barbarino," he declares. "This is my place. And these are my people."

Barbarino's speech pattern, as much as any other character in *Welcome Back, Kotter*, reeks of stereotypical Brooklynese. He pronounces "through" "tru" and "sure" "shuwah." If he spoke proper English, he would begin a sentence by saying "You were" or "We were." But instead, he says "You was" or "We was"—which comes out "Youse" and "Weez."

Kotter will win over the Sweathogs via comic asides, Groucho Marx imitations, and the knowledge that, a decade earlier, he was one of them. In that first episode, he catches Horshack reading a girlie magazine, at which point Barbarino quips. "Mr. Kotter. I have an idea. Why don't we take one of these chicks and put her up on the wall so our study group may study her?" Kotter one-ups Barbarino by staring at the magazine and "reading her biography." This episode also has Barbarino spouting such witticisms as "Up your nose with a rubber hose" and "Off my case, toilet face." Kotter bests him with lower-down and dirtier lines recalled from *his* time as a Sweathog.

That night, Kotter tells Julie that he is ready to quit teaching at Buchanan. "Thomas Wolfe was right," he says. "You can't go home again." But the Sweathogs—along with the first in a line of females who will appear as Barbarino's girlfriends—show up at the Kotters' apartment. This girl, who is unnamed, and unlisted in the credits, holds Barbarino's hand. She has a line, spoken as she looks at Barbarino admiringly: "Every so often Vinnie wants to marry me. Last time it was behind the billboards on 84th Street."

The Sweathogs have learned of Kotter's past relationship with Buchanan. After showing them a scrapbook from his student days at the school, he reconsiders his decision to leave—and a sitcom is born.

In the first episode, all four Sweathogs are given equal time on-camera. But after only a few episodes, Travolta became the audience favorite—and was to remain so for the run of the show. This is illustrated by a section in the April 1977 issue of *TV Superstar*, a teen-oriented fanzine. It is devoted to "Barbarino & the Sweathogs"—not "Kotter (or Horshack, Epstein, or Washington) & the Sweathogs."

During his first year as Barbarino, Travolta received more than two-hundred thousand fan letters. He only answered the first fifty, and eventually averaged ten thousand letters a week. "It's mostly from girls between the ages of thirteen and eighteen," Travolta reported in early 1976. "They write a great deal about love, some even offer marriage proposals. But I don't want to go into it any deeper than that and get myself into trouble. You can use your imagination."

Travolta was not being vainglorious. While playing Barbarino, thirty thousand fans showed up to greet him for a personal appearance at a Chicago-area supermarket. Reportedly he had to switch clothes with a police officer to escape without being mauled. Another ten thousand materialized for an appearance in Hicksville, Long Island. "I borrowed a policeman's cap and jacket to disguise myself and get away in Hicksville," he told columnist Earl Wilson.

During the *Welcome Back, Kotter* taping, under-eighteen girls reportedly had to be barred from the soundstage. It seemed that too many of them would scream in ecstasy when he came on the set. This unabashed popularity might have segued into a series toplining Travolta. The powers at ABC even approached him about doing a *Kotter* spin-off, but the project never materialized.

Barbarino's popularity was to equal that of Henry Winkler's Arthur "Fonzie" Fonzarelli, of *Happy Days*: another self-involved, super-cool but essentially lovable Italian-American adolescent hood. "Originally Vinnie was very slick and very tough," James Komack explained in 1977. "He was a bully and a con artist." Indeed, in the show's second episode, titled *The Election*, Barbarino runs for student body president; he tries to intimidate his fellow candidates, and his motto is "Vote for Vinnie and nobody gets hurt." As the show evolved, the character was softened to reflect the demeanor of the actor playing him. "Johnny has a very likable, sweet, and even soulful personality," continued Komack. "He has a very spiritual attitude, so we made Barbarino a devout Catholic. Because Johnny can play against Barbarino's conceits, he makes him an extremely vulnerable character."

During the run of the show, Travolta mirrored Komack's description of the character when he noted, "I love Barbarino. Particularly as he's developed. . . . In the pilot script Barbarino was described as the class leader who hoped one day to be head of the Mafia. I instantly knew the character, but I've managed to give him more dimension as we've gone along. He used to be just cool and tough, but now he cries and has a lot of emotions."

Kotter and the Sweathogs: Gabe Kaplan (center) and Travolta, Ron Palillo, Robert Hegyes, Lawrence-Hilton Jacobs (left to right).

Perhaps the most intriguing episode featuring Barbarino had him deciding to become a priest, as per the deathbed wish of his eighty-seven-year-old grandmother. Of course, any scenario involving a Sweathog has to be tempered with comedy, so Barbarino hands out religious tracts titled "Heaven on $5 a Day," "Judgment Day and What to Wear," and "Sermons for the Shower." Epstein's comment to him sums up the Sweathogs' attitude towards their leader's career choice: "It's Foo Foo Da Da time, Vin Vin."

Other story lines had serious overtones. One had one of Barbarino's teachers yelling at him, and then promptly dropping dead. The conscience-stricken Sweathog thinks he is guilty of murder, and turns himself in to the police. More often, though, Barbarino was a carefree character who would dance and sing. In one episode, he does the "Ba-ba-barino," a wild rock 'n roll routine modeled after the early 1960s classic, "Barbara-Ann." In another, he and his fellow Sweathogs form a singing

group called "Three Dos and a Don't" and enter a talent competition. With his pals singing backup, Barbarino solos in "Jeepers Creepers" both in falsetto and deep voice. At the finale of the number, he forms two of his fingers into the shape of a **V**. His hand then glides across his eyes: a gesture which Travolta was to repeat almost two decades later while dancing with Uma Thurman in *Pulp Fiction!*

Another career precursor occurs in an episode spotlighting a high school play. Travolta soon was to be cast in *Saturday Night Fever*, at which point critics would compare him to early Marlon Brando. At one juncture in the show, Barbarino rips off his shirt and cries out, "Stella! Stella!" He then drops to his knees and declares, "I coulda been a contender!"

Finally, Barbarino-related plots spotlight his endless relationships with the opposite sex. He becomes involved with different girls but also fears he has lost his sex appeal. In what is perhaps the greatest affront to his machismo, he becomes mortified after being slapped by a teacher in front of the girls' gym class.

"In no way are we alike," Travolta explained as *Kotter* was heating up the airwaves. "I was a clown in school, but I certainly was not a leader. I wasn't that tough. As for girls, maybe I'd have one girlfriend. But Vinnie has a lot. I wouldn't know how to handle them.

"Vinnie's interests are very different from mine. But I enjoy playing him. His point of view is hysterical, much more funny than my own personal view of life."

As the show settled into its run, the gossip columns reported that Travolta's huge popularity threatened to unseat the show's star, Gabe Kaplan (who also had helped develop the series with James Komack). Kaplan, however, denied these rumors. "I think John is a terrific actor and has helped the show immensely," Kaplan declared in 1977. "If there is anybody on the show I'm close to it's John. We're the best of friends. Despite his success, he's still the same as the day he first walked onto the show."

But the rumors persisted. In a classic piece of gossip-mongering published in the November 10, 1977 *New York Post*, Jason Winters wrote that "jealousy, flying tempers and John Travolta's apparent egotism have created a miserable atmosphere on the Hollywood soundstage where TV's *Welcome Back, Kotter* is taped." He added that "network concessions to Travolta seem partly responsible for the erosion of the cast's morale . . ." The key words in the piece are "apparent" and "seem partly responsible": the writer offered no conclusive proof that Travolta had turned into Attila the Hun. He also described Travolta's abilities as "limited," and referred to *Saturday Night Fever* and *Grease* as "two un-released films," as if to imply that they were not worthy of playing in movie houses.

Without offering a response from the Travolta camp, Winters reported that the actor "did not appear for the rehearsal of the season's opening segment, which was written around him, leaving the show's staff to rehearse alone until the threat of a multimillion-dollar law suit returned

While in the development stage, *Welcome Back, Kotter's* Sweathogs were modeled after The Dead End Kids (*opposite*, pictured with John Garfield and Gloria Dickson in *They Made Me a Criminal*) and the urban thugs in *Blackboard Jungle* (*above*, among whose minions were Sidney Poitier, Vic Morrow, Jamie Farr and Paul Mazursky).

him to work." He also observed that Ron Palillo's Horshack had become the most popular Sweathog, and that Gabe Kaplan "reportedly sees Palillo as a threat."

But Travolta still was a regular on *Welcome Back, Kotter* when *Saturday Night Fever* made him a movie star. At that time, *Kotter* and ABC needed him much more than he needed them. In January 1978, in order to spice up the show, a female Sweathog, Angie Globagoski (Melonie Haller), was added to the group. That fall, the beginning of the show's final season, a male Sweathog, Beau De Labarre (Stephen Shortridge), came on board. That season, Travolta appeared on just eight of the twenty-two *Kotter* episodes. In order to secure this arrangement, he had to battle the show's producers. His problem was neither his ego nor his salary, but his desire to have more time in which to appear in movies.

At the demise of *Welcome Back, Kotter* Travolta may have outgrown the confines of the small screen, but he was not quite through playing Barbarino. In 1994, upon the release of *Pulp Fiction*, he made his first appearance as guest host of *Saturday Night Live*. One of the skits is a *Kotter* parody, in which an episode of the show is presented as if it had been directed by Quentin Tarantino. Two *Reservoir Dogs / Pulp Fiction*-style gangsters arrive in Kotter's classroom; they are promptly blown away by Barbarino (Travolta) and his fellow Sweathogs, who are depicted as vicious, Tarantinoesque hoods.

Welcome Back, Kotter Videography

The show had its network premiere on September 9, 1975, and ran on ABC through August 10, 1979 (including repeats). In all, ninety-five separate programs were taped. *Kotter* first was scheduled on Tuesday evenings from 8:30 to 9:00. In January 1976, its time slot was switched to Thursday from 8:30 to 9:00; between September and October 1978, it was aired on Monday from 8:00 to 8:30; beginning in October 1978, it was moved to Saturday from 8:00 to 8:30; in February and March 1979, it was aired on

Saturday from 8:30 to 9:00; finally, between May 1979, and its cancellation, it was aired on Friday from 8:30 to 9:00.

Guest stars who appeared on *Welcome Back, Kotter* include James Woods (Episode 5), John Astin (Episode 26), Pat Morita (Episode 27), Harold J. Stone (Episode 41), and George Carlin (Episode 44). Garry Shandling authored Episode 37, *Horshack vs. Carvelli*. The latter character was played by Charles Fleischer, the future voice of Roger Rabbit.

Quite a few of the episode titles were take-offs on popular songs, television shows, books, and movies. Among the cleverest: *Sweatside Story, The Sweat Smell of Success, Sweatwork, Frog Day Afternoon, Beau's Jest, Come Back Little Arnold, Swine and Punishment,* and *One Flu Over the Cuckoo's Nest. Good-bye Mr. Chips* was reconstituted twice, as *Good-bye Mr. Kripps*—the episode in which Barbarino thinks he has murdered his teacher—and *Hello Ms. Chips.*

The final *Kotter* season begins with Episode 72. Travolta acted only in that episode and in numbers 74, 77, 80, 83, 85, 87, and 88.

Episode 1: *Welcome Back, Kotter*
The pilot episode.

Episode 2: *The Election*
Barbarino runs for student body president against two pupils he considers "overachievers."

Episode 3: *Basket Case*
Washington makes the varsity basketball team, and becomes uninterested in taking his exams.

Episode 4: *Whodunit?*
Rosalie "Hotsy" Totzi tells Gabe that she is pregnant, and he attempts to uncover the identity of the father.

Episode 5: *The Great Debate*
The Sweathogs go one-on-one against the school debating team.

Episode 6: *No More Mr. Nice Guy*
Mr. Woodman mellows after teaching the Sweathogs a history lesson. Meanwhile, Kotter becomes a disciplinarian.

Episode 7: *One of Our Sweathogs Is Missing*
Epstein disappears because he is humiliated after losing a fight.

Episode 8: *Classroom Marriage*
Epstein decides to marry, but Kotter convinces him to wait.

Episode 9: *Mr. Kotter Teacher*
Kotter is suspended from teaching by Mr. Woodman.

Episode 10: *Barbarino's Girl*
Barbarino received a poor report card, and Kotter persuades him to get a tutor.

Episode 11: *The Reunion*
Kotter evaluates his teaching career after a visit from his old pal, Lyle Flanagan.

Episode 12: *California Dreamin'*
The Sweathogs fawn over Bambi, a new student who claims to be from California, but she develops a crush on "Gabesy."

Episode 13: *Arrivederci, Arnold*
Horshack is promoted scholastically, but wants to remain with the Sweathogs.

Episode 14: *The Sit-in*
The Sweathogs stage a protest when they are served liver in the school cafeteria.

Episode 15: *The Longest Weekend*
Kotter gets lonely when Julie goes off skiing with a girlfriend.

Episode 16: *Doctor Epstein, I Presume?*
The school guidance counselor advises Epstein that he lacks the intelligence to become a veterinarian, so Epstein presents all his pets to Kotter.

Episode 17: *Follow the Leader, Part 1*
When Barbarino is dethroned as the Sweathogs' leader, he decides to quit school.

Episode 18: *Follow the Leader, Part 2*
Barbarino moves in with Kotter after Julie, fed up with her husband's preoccupation with the Sweathogs, moves into a hotel.

Episode 19: *One Flu Over the Cuckoo's Nest*
After a flu epidemic hits Buchanan, the schools' brighter students are mixed in with the Sweathogs.

Episode 20: *The Telethon*
In order to solicit money for their class, Kotter and the Sweathogs stage a telethon.

Episode 21: *Kotter Makes Good*
Kotter learns from Mr. Woodman that he never took his final exams as a Buchanan student.

Episode 22: *Father Vinnie*
Barbarino decides to become a priest, just as his grandmother requested on her deathbed.

Episode 23: *Sweatside Story*
Kotter steps in when the Sweathogs resolve to go into battle against a gang at rival New Utrecht High School.

Episode 24: *A Love Story*
Epstein becomes angry when his sister becomes a Sweathog and Barbarino asks her out.

Episode 25: *Gabe Under Pressure*
Kotter is not pleased at being coerced into taking a physical.

Episode 26: *The Museum*
Kotter and the Sweathogs become locked in a tomb with a mummy during a museum field trip.

Episode 27: *Career Day*
Kotter is offered a well-paying job in Chicago.

Episode 28: *Inherit the Halibut*
Class treasurer Washington is the prime suspect when the class fund is discovered missing.

Episode 29: *Sweathog Clinic for the Cure of Smoking*
Kotter and the Sweathogs assist Epstein when he decides to quit smoking.

Episode 30: *Chicken à la Kotter*
Kotter moonlights as a chicken in a fast-food restaurant.

Episode 31: *The Fight*
Bickering leaves the Sweathogs no longer on speaking terms.

Episode 32: *Sweathog, Nebraska Style*
Julie's out-of-town sister, visiting Brooklyn, promptly becomes a Sweathog, and starts dating Epstein.

Episode 33: *Sadie Hawkins Day*
Barbarino is the sole Sweathog without a date for the school dance.

Episode 34: *Hello Ms. Chips*
A student teacher discovers that teaching the Sweathogs is an experience

unlike anything she has learned in school.

Episode 35: *Whatever Happened to Arnold, Part 1*
Horshack has the lead in the school play, *Cyrano de Bergerac*, but quits the role and disappears when the Sweathogs tease him. He is replaced by Barbarino.

Episode 36: *Whatever Happened to Arnold, Part 2*
When his fifth father dies, Horshack decides to become head of the household. (This episode was the pilot for a prospective series featuring Horshack and his family.)

Episode 37: *Horshack vs. Carvelli*
Horshack agrees to fight Carvelli, the toughest punk at New Utrecht High School.

Episode 38: *Hark, the Sweatkings*
The Sweathogs befriend and attempt to reform a neighborhood bum.

Episode 39: *Sweatgate Scandal*
The Sweathogs become reporters for the school newspaper and unearth a scandal in the cafeteria.

Episode 40: *Caruso's Way*
Barbarino is mortified after the physical education teacher hits him in front of the girls' gym class.

Episode 41: *Kotter & Son*
Kotter's father visits from Florida.

Episode 42: *The Littlest Sweathog*
Kotter is delighted by the news that Julie is pregnant, but she is uncertain if she is ready for motherhood.

Episode 43: *I'm Having Their Baby*
While Kotter attends a teacher's convention, the Sweathogs attempt to cheer a depressed Julie.

Episode 44: *Radio Free Freddie*
Washington wins fame as a deejay on station WBAD.

Episode 45: *I Wonder Who's Kissing Gabe Now*
The school art teacher falls for Kotter, and the Sweathogs believe they are having an affair.

Episode 46: *And Baby Makes Four, Part 1*
The Sweathogs—except for Barbarino—graduate to eleventh grade, and Julie is about to become a mother.

Episode 47: *And Baby Makes Four, Part 2*
Gabe and Julie become the parents of twin daughters, while Barbarino

pesters him to get him out of the tenth grade.

Episode 48: *And Baby Makes Four, Part 3*
The Kotters bring the babies home to utter chaos.

Episode 49: *Buddy, Can You Spare a Million*
Kotter and Barbarino quarrel over a lottery ticket.

Episode 50: *Just Testing*
Kotter ponders whether to help Barbarino prepare for a makeup test or spend time with his family.

Episode 51: *The De-Programming of Arnold Horshack*
Horshack finds acceptance after joining the "Ba Ba Bee Bee" religious cult, but the Sweathogs disapprove.

Episode 52: *What a Move!*
Epstein assists the Kotters in finding a larger apartment.

Episode 53: *A Novel Idea*
The Sweathogs are not amused when Mr. Woodman authors a novel in which they are parodied.

Episode 54: *Barbarino in Love, Part 1*
Barbarino falls in love with Cassy, one of the Sweathogs' competitors in the state finals talent contest.

Episode 55: *Barbarino in Love, Part 2*
Barbarino thinks he must choose between Cassy and winning the contest.

Episode 56: *Kotter for Vice-Principal*
Kotter may be appointed Buchanan's new vice-principal.

Episode 57: *Swine and Punishment*
Washington is accused by Mr. Woodman of cheating on an exam.

Episode 58: *Epstein's Madonna*
Epstein the artist paints a nude woman whose face is that of Julie.

Episode 59: *Angie*
Chaos ensues when Angie, a new girl in school, wants to become a Sweathog.

Episode 60: *Sweatwork*
Low ratings lead to Horshack's imminent firing from the school radio station.

Episode 61: *Meet Your New Teacher: Batteries Not Included*
A computer threatens to displace Kotter.

Episode 62: *Epstein's Term Paper*
Epstein purchases bogus term papers from Carvelli, unaware that one was

"authored" a decade earlier by Kotter.

Episode 63: *There's No Business, Part 1*
Kotter successfully auditions at a comedy club, and has the chance to become a professional comedian.

Episode 64: *There's No Business, Part 2*
Kotter switches professions, leaving Julie and the Sweathogs without a husband and a teacher.

Episode 65: *What Goes Up*
Kotter and the Sweathogs come to the rescue when Washington becomes addicted to pills.

Episode 66: *Good-bye Mr. Kripps*
A teacher drops dead after yelling at Barbarino, who thinks he is guilty of murder.

Episode 67: *Horshack and Madame X*
Horshack becomes enamored of Julie.

Episode 68: *The Kiss*
Kotter offers artificial respiration to a girl who has fainted, and then is denounced for kissing her.

Episode 69: *Class Encounters of the Carvelli Kind*
Carvelli comes in contact with a UFO, and Mr. Woodman has been selected to join him on an otherworldly journey.

Episode 70: *The Return of Hotsy Totzi*
The Sweathogs discover that Hotsy Totzi is a mother—and an exotic dancer.

Episode 71: *Sweathog Christmas Special*
The Sweathogs reminisce as they celebrate Christmas with the Kotters.

Episode 72: *Sweathog Back to School Special*
A new semester begins, and Kotter and the Sweathogs remember events from previous years.

Episode 73: *The Drop-ins, Part 1*
Mr. Woodman becomes the Buchanan principal, Kotter is the new vice-principal, and the Sweathogs want to quit school.

Episode 74: *The Drop-ins, Part 2*
The Sweathogs come to understand that they lack the education and experience to secure jobs.

Episode 75: *Frog Day Afternoon*
Horshack goes on a "Save the Frog" kick after refusing to participate in a biology class dissection.

Episode 76: *Beau's Jest*

New Sweathog Beau plays a joke on Epstein by setting him up on a date with a married woman.

Episode 77: *The Sweatmobile*
The Sweathogs purchase a car.

Episode 78: *Don't Come Up and See Me Sometime*
Barbarino's attitude toward the Sweathogs changes after he gets his own apartment.

Episode 79: *Once Upon a Ledge*
Horshack comes to the rescue when a Buchanan student attempts to commit suicide.

Episode 80: *Barbarino's Boo-Boo*
Mr. Woodman enters the hospital for a bunion operation, and Barbarino manages to "lose" him.

Episode 81: *Washington's Clone*
An "A" student is determined to become a Sweathog, and emulate Washington.

Episode 82: *X-Rated Education*
Epstein unwittingly replaces the sex education film that Julie has arranged for a parents' group with an X-rated movie.

Episode 83: *The Barbarino Blues*
Barbarino thinks he has lost his appeal to women.

Episode 84: *A Little Fright Music*
Washington wants to pen a new Buchanan school song.

Episode 85: *Bride and Gloom*
Barbarino becomes determined to get married.

Episode 86: *The Good-bye Guy*
Epstein intends to live with Mr. Woodman's niece.

Episode 87: *A Winter's Coat Tale*
Barbarino's new coat is stolen.

Episode 88: *Barbarino's Baby*
Barbarino is stuck in an elevator, where he delivers a baby.

Episode 89: *The Sweat Smell of Success*
Epstein transforms the staid school paper into a scandal sheet.

Episode 90: *I'm Okay, But You're Not*
Beau's attempt to butter up Mr. Woodman backfires when the Sweathogs accuse him of backstabbing.

Episode 91: *The Gang Show*

Epstein and Washington aspire to be the school talent contest winners.

Episode 92: *Come Back Little Arnold*
Horshack takes to the bottle in order to gain confidence with his girl-friend.

Episode 93: *OO-OO, I Do, Part 1*
Horshack learns that he may be transferred to another school just as he and his girlfriend are getting serious.

Episode 94: *OO-OO, I Do, Part 2*
The Sweathogs give Horshack a bachelor party that results in disaster.

Episode 95: *The Bread Winners*
Epstein interviews for a job, only to learn that it already has been taken by Washington.

While none of the other *Welcome Back, Kotter* cast members went on to enjoy a success to rival Travolta's, neither did they fade from the planet. Ron Palillo became a children's book illustrator, and acted in movies and on television. In the mid-1980s, he was the voice of Rubik on *Rubik the Amazing Cube*, an animated series based on the popular puzzle; in the 1990s, he appeared for ten months on the soap opera *One Life to Live*. Between 1986 and 1988, Robert Hegyes played Detective Manny Esposito on *Cagney & Lacey*, and has been a visiting professor at Rowan College in New Jersey. Lawrence-Hilton Jacobs's credits include the mini-series *Roots*, the made-for-TV movie *Michael Jackson: An American Dream*, and the syndicated series *Pointman*. Marcia Strassman, who earlier had appeared as Nurse Margie Cutler on *M*A*S*H*, did other series work, including *Booker* (a *21 Jump Street* spin-off, aired during the 1989–90 season, in which she played Alice Rudd); the short-lived *Good Time Harry*, as sportswriter Carol Younger; and the pilot of the first, less-successful show titled *E/R*, a 1984 sitcom featuring Elliott Gould. In the last, she was cast as Dr. Eve Sheridan, a role played in the series by Mary McDonnell.

Strassman also costarred with Rick Moranis in the popular Disney comedy-fantasies *Honey, I Shrunk the Kids* and *Honey, I Blew Up the Kid*. Finally, Gabe Kaplan did stand-up comedy in Las Vegas, and starred as a New Yorker transplanted to Nevada in the theatrical feature *Fast Break* and a New Yorker transplanted to Texas in the short-lived sitcom *Lewis & Clark*. He also toured in a one-man show as Groucho Marx. Eventually he lost interest in show business and settled into an eighteen-room mansion in Los Angeles, where he oversees his own lucrative investment portfolio.

John Travolta, pin-up handsome, during the latter stages of his run on *Welcome Back, Kotter*.

In May 1995—in the wake of Travolta's stunning career rebound in *Pulp Fiction*—Nickelodeon, the cable television network whose evening programming specializes in classic TV series, began airing episodes of *Welcome Back, Kotter*. The show settled comfortably into an 11 P.M. time slot, making it an alternative for viewers uninterested in watching their local news or too politically correct to watch *Politically Incorrect* on the Comedy Channel.

"We think this show will have a real appeal to twenty- and-thirtysomethings," observed Rick Cronin, the station's general manager. "It has the same sort of appeal as *The Brady Bunch*. It's a show people remember.

"This was when America discovered John Travolta."

Travolta: Teen Fave

To 1970s mothers who had conveniently forgotten how they once had squealed over Elvis the Pelvis, he may have been "John Revolta." But to their Barbarino-crazed teenybopper daughters, John Travolta was an honest-to-goodness heartthrob.

And he was exploited as such. The cover of the May 1976 issue of *Tiger Beat* magazine enticed its young readers by running a photo of a dreamy-looking Travolta along with a headline informing them that JOHN "BARBARINO" TRAVOLTA WANTS YOUR PHONE NUMBER—WILL YOU GIVE IT TO HIM?

Readers of the April 1977 issue of *TV Superstar* were given the lowdown on their hero in JOHN TRAVOLTA FROM A TO Z! WHAT MAKES HIM SO SEXY! Among the tidbits: "A is for attractive. Whether he's in a tuxedo or jeans, John always manages to look absolutely outasight"; "B is for blue eyes no girl can resist! Whether sparkling with happiness or flashing in anger, they hypnotize"; "C is for cool and John has plenty! He's a super guy who always knows just what to say at the right place and time" . . . all the way to "Z brings to mind zest. John is full of enthusiasm and joy for living. He's one high school dropout who turned his life around."

Adolescent girls were meant to be titillated by a piece in the November 1977 *Teen Pin-Ups*, in which they were challenged to pass Travolta's "Kissing Test." Prior to the questions, they were enticed by copy which began, "Imagine John Travolta's handsome face coming closer and closer to yours, his lips moving toward you, his blue eyes looking deep into your eyes. Imagine his lips touching your lips, so softly, so tenderly. You close your eyes and drift into the wonderful dreamworld of that moment, and you wish it could last forever . . ."

The actor's teen-mag hype was linked to his starring in *Saturday Night Fever* and *Grease*. The May 1978 *Photoplay* featured a shaggy-haired Travolta on the cover, along with smaller photos of *Fever* actresses Karen Lynn Gorney and Donna Pescow and *Grease* costar Olivia Newton-

28 at bottom

28

4 PAGES OF CENTER GALLERY COLOR PIN-UPS FROM "GREASE!"

12 FULL PAGES OF COLOR: TRAVOLTA, OLIVIA, FRAMPTON, ANDY GIBB & BEE GEES!

TV Stars today

SEPTEMBER 1978

02793 $1.25

BEE GEES & FRAMPTON PHOTO ALBUM FROM SGT. PEPPER!

TRAVOLTA & OLIVIA PHOTO ALBUM FROM GREASE!

MEET ANDY GIBB: PLUS EXCLUSIVE ELVIS TRIBUTE!

John. Readers were promised that they would learn WHAT JOHN GIVES GIRLS TO MAKE THEM LOVE HIM. *Grooves Presents Travolta*, which hit newsstands two months later, was devoted entirely to you-know-who. According to its cover, it included OUTRAGEOUS COLOR PINUPS and HUNDREDS OF INTIMATE FACTS & PIX as well as revealing data on THE MAKING OF A SUPERSTAR: HIS LIFE, LOVES, TRIUMPHS—AND HEARTBREAK, and JOHN'S PERFECT STARMATE: IS IT VALERIE BERTINELLI, KATE JACKSON, CINDY WILLIAMS, LINDA RONSTADT, DEBBY BOONE, MARIE OSMOND—OR *YOU*?

 TV Stars Today even sponsored "The Official John Travolta Fan Club." For $10, a panting Travolta lover would receive her very own "personal two-year membership" in the club. Perks included a "special, exclusive, personal 45 RPM recording of John's voice"; "11 Exclusive, Never Before Seen Full Color Photos with John's signature"; a "personal Membership Card" with "Matching Membership Card Holder"; a "Full Color Membership Folder"; a "Special, Personal Welcoming letter from John"; and an "Exclusive, Complete Biography giving you *all* the most important facts about John." If you were not in the $10 allowance bracket, $5 would get you "all of the sensational items in the Membership Kit" minus the record of Travolta's voice.

 At the height of his popularity in *Welcome Back, Kotter, Saturday Night Fever*, and *Grease*, Travolta became one of his generation's premiere pinup boys. He was posed as Valentino. He was photographed in boxing

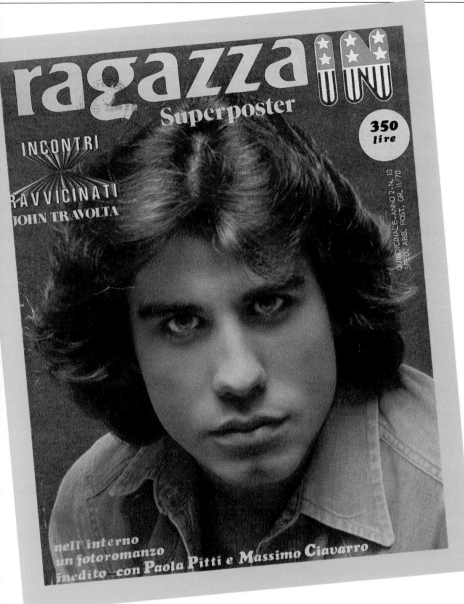

ragazza **IN**

Superposter

350 *lire*

INCONTRI

RAVVICINATI
JOHN TRAVOLTA

QUINDICINALE-ANNO 2-N.13
SPED. ABB. POST. GR. II/70

*nell' interno
un fotoromanzo
inedito con Paola Pitti e Massimo Ciavarro*

Travolta's popularity was world-wide, as witnessed by this Italian-produced "Superposter"

gloves. He was endlessly pictured simply looking dreamy and cute, with his dimple and smile meant to elicit oohs and aahs from the teenybopper throngs. He remained a teen magazine staple until he was past his thirtieth birthday. In the February 1984 issue of *Teen Beat*, he is pictured on the cover along with much-younger adolescent heartthrobs Tom Cruise, Rob Lowe, and C. Thomas Howell. The article inside hypes *Two of a Kind*, his reunion movie with *Grease* costar Olivia Newton-John.

In 1978, Travolta was first listed in *Who's Who in America*—at the same time that the East German communist government characterized him as being a pawn in a capitalistic scheme to brainwash the world's teenagers! According to *Junge Welt*, the country's government-edited youth newspaper, "Travolta tries to make capitalistic daily life seem harmless." The following year, Soviet journalist Yuri Borovoi wrote in the *Literaturnaya Gazeta* that Travolta's star had permanently faded. "Only one joy is left to him—the childish habit of gluing together brightly colored model airplanes," Borovoi wrote of the "former star." A drawing accompanying the piece depicted Travolta as a puppet.

Four

Travolta Ephemera

At age twenty-two, most young actors are waiting tables, scurrying to classes and auditions, and crossing their fingers that success will someday be theirs. But when Travolta was twenty-two, he already had won national popularity on *Welcome Back, Kotter*; even more acclaim was to come his way as the star of *Saturday Night Fever* and *Grease*.

As such, he was transformed into a mini-cottage industry. His handlers included more than just his agents. The accounting firm of Gelfand, Breslauer, Macnow, Rennert & Feldman managed his business activities. The law firm of Bushkin, Kopelson, Gaims & Gaines handled his legal affairs. He had his own director of public relations, Michele Cohen. He had a slew of advisers, managers, and mentors. And he was much more than a teenybopper hero-turned-movie star. He was a marketable commodity, who could be sold to the public in a variety of guises.

Perhaps the most intriguing of all 1970s Travolta ephemera is a twelve-inch John Travolta doll, marketed by Chem Toy, with "bendable legs" and a "movable waist." The doll is "poseable," and "can wear clothes of Ken, Donnie, and all other twelve-inch dolls."

Other items relating directly to Travolta include Revell's "firebird fever" model kit, a GAF Viewmaster, and "The Official John Travolta Picture/Postcard Book," which includes "23 gorgeous photos in full color." Fanzine-style books were published, including *John Travolta*, by Cary Schumacher; *John Travolta: Making an Impact*, by Linda Jacobs; *John Travolta: Super Sensation of the Seventies!*, by Suzanne Munshower; and *The John Travolta Scrapbook: An Illustrated Biography*, also by Munshower.

In addition to the likes of *Tiger Beat* and *Photoplay*, Travolta found himself featured in —if not on the cover of—an array of magazines, from *Attenzione* to *TV Guide*, *Rolling Stone* to *Time*, *Dance Magazine* to *Films in Review*. In July 1978, he became the first male to appear all by himself on the cover in the 102-year history of *McCall's* magazine.

The young superstar found his name on books not completely related to him. Rex Reed published a compilation of celebrity interviews titled *Travolta to Keaton*. Harold J. Kennedy, the director of Travolta's summer theater production of *Bus Stop*, penned a reminiscence called *No Pickle, No Performance: An Irreverent Theatrical Excursion From Tallulah to Travolta*.

Still other Travolta paraphernalia are offshoots of *Welcome Back, Kotter*, *Saturday Night Fever*, and *Grease*. You could have your breakfast-in-bed served on a *Kotter* tray. You could carry your midday meal to school—or work, if like Tony Manero you already had become a nine-to-five wage slave—in a variety of *Kotter* lunchboxes. You could play with your very own *Kotter* paper dolls (advertised as offering HOURS OF FUN FOR BOYS AND GIRLS AGES 4 AND OVER), color forms or "Sweat Hogs car," and save your pennies by storing them in a "Sweat Hogs bank." If *War and Peace* or *Ulysses* were too heady for your literary tastes, you could thumb through the pages of your "DC TV" *Welcome Back, Kotter* comic books.

If you were Barbarino-crazed, you could have your very own Mattel eight-inch-high "Barbarino figure" (among other dolls depicting *Kotter* characters, all of which could be placed inside a portable vinyl classroom).

You and your friends could play board games based on *Welcome Back, Kotter*, *Saturday Night Fever*, and *Grease*. You could collect trading cards—and, if you were from Brooklyn, you even could flip them—depicting scenes from *Kotter*, *Fever*, and *Grease*. When you wearied of fiddling with these items, you could toss them into your official *Welcome Back, Kotter* and *Saturday Night Fever* trash cans. And you could pass the wee hours of the night pining for your hero as you thumbed through the *Saturday Night Fever Official Authorized Scrapbook*, which came "packed with exclusive photos."

Travolta also influenced mens' fashion. Upon the release of *Saturday Night Fever*, three-piece white polyester suits became the rage

PLOT-YOUR-OWN ADVENTURE STORIES™

STAYING ALIVE

From the
Paramount hit movie
starring John Travolta!

by William Rotsler

GREASE 1 ™
Danny and Sandy
© 1978 PARAMOUNT PICTURES CORPORATION

THE SWEAT HOGS IN THEIR OWN COMIC!

30¢ NO. 1 NOV. 30722

NEW WELCOME BACK, KOTTER

YOU *DON'T* UNDERSTAND, MR. WOODMAN!

THIS *IS* THE SOCIAL STUDIES CLASS!

REMEDIAL COLORING BOOK

BONUS! EVERYTHING YOU WANTED TO KNOW ABOUT... GABRIEL KAPLAN!

for hip young disco mavens, and barber shops began advertising Travolta-style haircuts. His mode of dress in *Urban Cowboy* helped ignite a country-western fashion craze.

In 1979, film critic Gene Siskel purchased the white three-piece suit and black shirt Travolta wore in *Saturday Night Fever* for $2,000 at a charity auction. One of those he outbid was Jane Fonda. In 1995, the suit was sold at auction to an unknown buyer for $145,500. One of the other bidders was Turner Network Television, owned by Ted Turner, who had become Fonda's husband. TNT dropped out of the bidding at $55,000. The *New York Times* quoted the auctioneer as declaring that the price was "certainly a record for polyester."

However, also in 1995, Travolta's black *Grease* jacket was sold at auction— for a measly $6,900!

Five

Travolta on Record

After singing on one of the episodes of *Welcome, Back, Kotter*, Travolta was enticed into signing a contract with the Midland International label, a division of RCA Records. His biggest hit came in 1976 with "Let Her In," which sold 800,000 copies, lasting twenty weeks on the *Billboard* pop chart and peaking at number ten. That same year, he sang "Whenever I'm Away From You" (six weeks, number thirty-eight). In 1977 came "All Strung Out on You" (eight weeks, number thirty-four). He also released two albums, *John Travolta* (1976) and *Can't Let You Go* (1977), both of which were reissued in 1978 as *Travolta Fever*. That same year, Midsong International, another RCA affiliate, released a twelve-inch disco single of Travolta singing "A Girl Like You."

As promising pop artists had done for decades, Travolta guested on Dick Clark's *American Bandstand*. In one such appearance, he is garbed in a tight-fitting red turtleneck with a gold chain around his neck. His hair is shoulder-length, with a nice wave. He is oh, so cute, and he looks like the soul brother of Shaun and David Cassidy. Another musical performance came on the Second Rock Music Awards show, which aired live from the Hollywood Palladium.

A clip of Travolta was included in *American Bandstand's 25th Anniversary Special*, which aired in 1977. He is featured in a section spotlighting what Clark described as "a very select group of young men who used to be the heartthrobs of *American Bandstand*'s female audience . . ." They included Paul Anka, Bobby Rydell, Rick Nelson, Frankie Lymon, Frankie Avalon, Pat Boone, Bobby Vee, Johnny Tillotson, The Osmonds, Paul Revere and the Raiders, and young Michael Jackson (appearing with the Jackson 5).

Travolta-the-singing-star also was popular abroad. In 1978, "Let Her In" and another single, "Sandy," became Top Twenty hits in England. "The Grease Megamix" became a Top Twenty hit there around Christmas 1990. Other Travolta recordings include the original

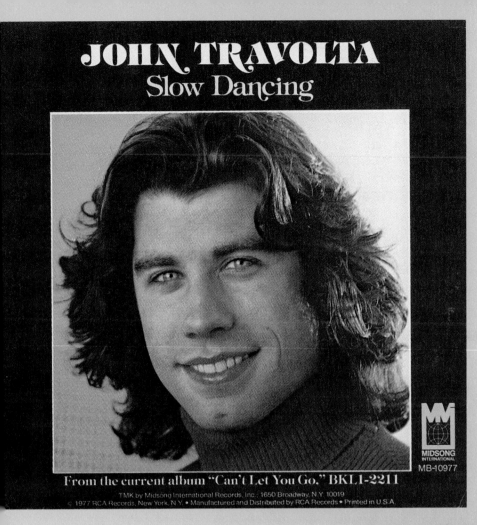

soundtrack of *Grease,* a 1978 best-seller; *Broadway Magic Vol. 2: The Great Performances*, a 1980 LP featuring performances by Angela Lansbury, Barbra Streisand, Julie Andrews, Richard Burton, and others, including Travolta in his "Dream Drummin'" number from *Over Here!*; *John Travolta,* an audio cassette released in Italy in 1981; and *Two of a Kind: Music From the Original Motion Picture Soundtrack* in 1983, in which he duets with Olivia Newton-John on "Take a Chance." In 1995, upon the release of *Pulp Fiction,* a British company, Charly Records, reissued twenty recordings Travolta made between 1976 and 1979 as a CD entitled *John Travolta: Greased Lightnin'.*

However, Travolta's biggest record successes were his *Grease* duets

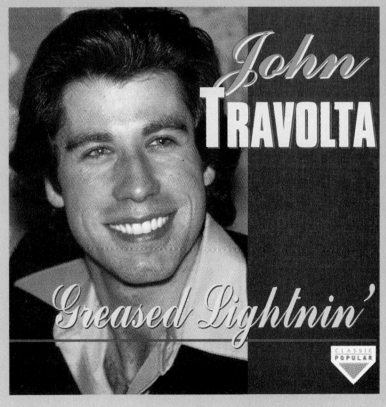

with Olivia Newton-John, all of which were released on the RSO label in 1978. "You're the One That I Want" enjoyed a twenty-four-week run on the *Billboard* Hot 100 pop charts, during which time it became a number one hit. "Summer Nights" made the charts for sixteen weeks, rising to number five. "Greased Lightnin'" (without Newton-John, in which he sang with Jeff Conaway) made the survey for eight weeks, peaking at number forty-seven.

Six

First Films . . . First Love

The Devil's Rain 1975

Bryanston. Director: Robert Fuest. Producers: James V. Cullen and
Michael S. Glick. Screenplay: Gabe Essoe, James Ashton, and Gerald
Hopman. Cinematographer: Alex Phillips Jr. Music: Al De Lory.
Editor: Michael Kahn. CAST: Ernest Borgnine *(Corbis)*, Eddie Albert *(Dr.
Richards)*, Ida Lupino *(Mrs. Preston)*, William Shatner *(Mark Preston)*,
Keenan Wynn *(Sheriff Owens)*, Tom Skerritt *(Tom Preston)*, Joan Prather
(*Julie Preston*), Woodrow Chambliss *(John)*, John Travolta *(Danny)*.
85 minutes. Rated: PG.

The Boy in the Plastic Bubble 1976

ABC-TV. Director: Randal Kleiser. Producers: Joel Thurm and Cindy
Dunne. Teleplay: Douglas Day Stewart, from the story by Stewart and
Joseph Morgenstern. Cinematographer: Arch R. Dalzell. Music: Mark
Snow. Editor: John F. McSweeney. CAST: John Travolta *(Tod Lubitch)*,
Glynnis O'Connor *(Gina Biggs)*, Robert Reed *(Johnny Lubitch)*, Diana
Hyland *(Mickey Lubitch)*, Ralph Bellamy *(Dr. Ernest Gunther)*, Karen
Morrow *(Martha Biggs)*, Howard Platt *(Pete Biggs)*, John Friedrich *(Roy
Slater)*, Vernee Watson *(Gwen)*, Edwin A. "Buzz" Aldrin *(Himself)*, Kelly
Ward *(Tom Shuster)*, Skip Lowell *(Bruce Shuster),* John Megna *(Smith)*,
Darrell Zwerling *(Mr. Brister)*, P. J. Soles *(Deborah)*.
100 minutes.

Carrie 1976

United Artists. Director: Brian De Palma. Producer: Paul Monash.
Screenplay: Lawrence D. Cohen, based on the novel by Stephen King.
Cinematographer: Mario Tosi. Music: Pino Donaggio. Editor: Paul
Hirsch. CAST: Sissy Spacek *(Carrie White)*, Piper Laurie *(Margaret White)*,
Amy Irving *(Sue Snell)*, William Katt *(Tommy Ross)*, Nancy Allen *(Chris
Hargenson)*, John Travolta *(Billy Nolan)*, Betty Buckley *(Miss Collins)*, P. J.
Soles *(Norma Watson)*, Sydney Lassick *(Mr. Fromm)*, Stefan Gierash
(Principal Morton), Priscilla Pointer *(Mrs. Snell)*.
97 minutes. Rated: R.

The "official" word on Travolta is that his first screen role came in *Carrie*. It says so in the press kits for *Get Shorty* and *White Man's Burden*, his first two post–*Pulp Fiction* releases. Even as far back as 1981, in the press kit for *Blow Out*, it is stated that Travolta was reunited with the film's director, Brian De Palma, "who also directed him in his motion picture debut, *Carrie*."

Yet Travolta had previously had a small role in *The Devil's Rain*, a tired, undistinguished Mexico-filmed horror opus involving a satanic cult. In it, he gets to utter the lines, "Blasphemer! Get him, he is a blasphemer!" At the finale, his character, Danny, literally melts during the title precipitation.

In *Carrie*, his role is strictly a plot device: Billy Nolan, the low-class boyfriend of pretty but venal, stubborn Chris Hargenson (Nancy Allen). Chris takes sadistic pleasure in taunting Carrie White (Sissy Spacek), a repressed high school student who is lorded over by a warped, religious fanatic mother (Piper Laurie)—and who also has telekinetic powers. Chris recruits Billy in a crude, cruel scheme that results in the dumping of a bucket of pig's blood over Carrie at the senior prom. In retaliation, Carrie employs her telekinesis, turning the prom into a holocaust and, later on, instigating Billy and Chris's grisly fate as their car crashes and burns.

The Boy in the Plastic Bubble easily is Travolta's most important pre–*Saturday Night Fever* movie credit. It offered evidence that Travolta was a multidimensional performer capable of transcending his Barbarino persona. In this made-for-television feature directed by Randal Kleiser (who later was to direct Travolta on the big screen in *Grease*), he played an adolescent wholly unlike Vinnie Barbarino or Tony Manero.

The scenario opens in 1959. Johnny and Mickey Lubitch (Robert Reed and Diana Hyland), a young married couple, learn that they are about to become parents. Even though they love children, they are less than overjoyed. "I don't want to lose another baby," Mickey cries. "I couldn't bear it. I just couldn't." Johnny consoles her by observing, "No way in the world we're gonna lose this child. Look, first of all, the odds are four-to-one against there being any problem at all this time . . ." He adds, "There were never two people in the world more meant to be parents than you and me. God knows that."

Johnny and Mickey do become parents, but not without much heartbreak. Tod, their son, enters the world via cesarean section and (as his doctor explains) "with no immunities whatsoever." "Until we discover a treatment [or] until he develops an immune system of his own," he tells the couple, "he'll have to remain in his protective environment." How long will that be? Days? Weeks? Months? "Years," is the medic's reply.

A beaming Travolta and his equally happy but ill-fated lady-love, Diana Hyland

And so is born the "boy in the plastic bubble."

The film goes on to detail how Johnny and Mickey struggle with their situation. But the crux of the story chronicles the teenage Tod (Travolta) and how he endures in his bubble, with a special focus on his growing relationship with Gina (Glynnis O'Connor), his nubile next-door neighbor. At first Gina thinks Tod is "weird," but he has fallen in love with her and wants her to see that he is "not a cripple." During the course of the film, her affection for him grows.

There are hints of Barbarino in Tod, as he goofs around while taking a class at the local high school via closed-circuit television. But the character's vulnerability, an offshoot of his unusual situation, is the overriding emotion at play here. Tod Lubitch is a difficult, emotionally complex character, and he is sensitively played by Travolta.

The only sequence in the film which does not ring true is the

Diana Hyland, in the 1960s.

final one. Tod and Gina have graduated from high school, and Gina soon will be leaving for New York to study art at Pratt Institute. One evening, Tod peers out his window and sees Gina tying up her horse. He knows that if he leaves his bubble he might die instantly—or, if not, he could be done in by a simple cold. At the same time, he may already have built up enough immunities so that he could survive on his own. Tod decides the time has come to find out. He leaves his bubble, as his parents sleep in their nearby bedroom, and for the first time breathes fresh air. This being a show which must have a happy ending, Tod does not keel over. Instead, he walks around. He touches a bush in front of his house, and then the bottom of a tree. He approaches Gina, who is brushing her horse's mane, and caresses her face. "Oh, so much softer than I ever imagined," he says. He kisses her, and then asks her to take him for a ride on her horse. (*The Boy in the Plastic Bubble* was based on the real life of a boy named David, who died several years after the film's production.)

Playing Tod's mother is a forty-year-old actress named Diana Hyland. A native of Cleveland Heights, Ohio, and a friend of Travolta's sister Ellen, the coolly elegant beauty had appeared on various TV series from the early 1960s through mid 1970s, including *The Fugitive*, *The Man From U.N.C.L.E.*, *Gunsmoke*, and *Kojak*. She was a regular on *Peyton Place* during the 1968–69 season. Her screen credits included *One Man's Way*, *The Chase*, and *Jigsaw*. She was a divorced, single parent, with a four-year-old son named Zachary.

During the course of the filming, Hyland and Travolta, who was then twenty-two, developed a friendship. In 1983, he admitted his attraction to her at their first meeting. "I saw the whole picture in her first ten words," he recalled, "depth, intelligence, beauty, perceptiveness." At the cast party, each acknowledged that their feelings transcended mere companionship. Soon, they were romantically involved. But the Travolta-Hyland relationship was fated to be tragically brief: within a year, the actress died of cancer. Today, it is especially heartbreaking watching *The Boy in the Plastic Bubble*, a story about illness, if you know the extent of Hyland's and Travolta's involvement, coupled with the actress's fate.

Hyland previously had had a mastectomy, and mistakenly thought she had survived the disease. Before her death, on March 27, 1977, Hyland had filmed the first four episodes of the TV series *Eight Is Enough*, playing Joan Bradford. Her character's husband (Dick Van Patten) was summarily made into a widower who subsequently married schoolteacher Sandra Sue "Abby" Abbott (Betty Buckley, who had played a sympathetic gym teacher in *Carrie*).

It was Hyland who encouraged Travolta to accept the role of Tony Manero in *Saturday Night Fever*. He was aware of the extent of her illness, but told no one. On the day before her death, he was in New York filming *Fever*. When it appeared that her demise was imminent, he flew back to California to be at her bedside. Also present at her death were her parents, TV husband Dick Van Patten, and Van Patten's wife, Pat. Several days later, Travolta returned to New York to continue playing Tony Manero, and he completed the film while experiencing a deep sense of mourning over his lost love. Travolta explained, soon after Hyland's death, "I felt the breath go out of her when she died in my arms. The eighteen-year gap in our ages never made any difference. . . . Part of me was ripped away when she was taken from me." Later on, he observed, "I would have married Diana. I would have been over the moon if we had had a baby."

Van Patten noted, soon after the tragedy, "Even though she was much older than Travolta it was a good relationship. They really were in love with each other. He idolized her and her little boy. . . . Frankly, I'm glad she had a lovely romance before she died. . . . All the time John never left her side [on the day she died]. He may be only in his twenties, but he's a real man."

Travolta had purchased a fashionable white suit, for a Rio de Janeiro vacation he had planned with Hyland. Instead, he wore it to her funeral.

Later in 1977, at a Malibu party hosted by *Grease* coproducer Allan Carr, Travolta observed, "Diana gave me the happiest nine months of my life. We were genuinely, completely in love. No woman will ever make me as happy as Diana did. I will never forget her." As he spoke, tears welled up in his eyes. At the end of the year, he acknowledged that "the pain of her death rubbed off in my performance" as Tony Manero.

"He was devastated not only by the loss but because there was nothing he could do," reported his sister Ellen. "Until Diana's death, John felt in control of his own fate and had never experienced anything tragic. He suddenly felt helpless, aware of his own mortality. Later he confided, 'If Diana can do it, so can I.' It made him lose his fear of death."

Hyland went on to win an Emmy for Outstanding Single Performance by a Supporting Actress in a Comedy or Drama Special, for her role in *The Boy in the Plastic Bubble*. The award ceremony took place September 12, 1977, a scant five-plus months after Hyland's death. Travolta attended, escorting Mr. and Mrs. John Gentner, Hyland's parents. One of the highlights of the show, as described by Morrie Gelman in *Variety*, was "John Travolta's bounding in the air when the late Diana Hyland was announced as the winner of a supporting actress award." He accepted for her, exclaiming, "Here's to you, Diana, wherever you are!" Eighteen years later—when Travolta was approaching Hyland's age at the time of her death—this first love continued to have a special place in his thoughts. "I loved Diana," he declared in an interview. "I mean, she's someone I miss."

Tragedy was to further taint Travolta's life when his beloved mother Helen died of cancer not long after Hyland. Helen Travolta, sixty-six, passed away on December 3, 1978. (Travolta's father, Salvatore, died of a heart ailment on May 29, 1995, at age eighty-two, just when his son was basking in the success of *Pulp Fiction*.) So at the same time that he was scaling the heights of a fame that any young actor would envy, Travolta was reeling from a double dose of personal calamity. "A night never goes by when there isn't one of them in some part of a dream," he revealed in 1980.

"It was a rude awakening that we are always right next to death," Travolta said three years later. "It's a cliché, but it gave me an ability to appreciate life more and to do things I want to do within reason." He added, "And I savor people more. I anticipate how much I'm going to miss them if they or I go. I'm less afraid of dying because I accept it more as a part of life."

Despite his presence in *The Devil's Rain*, Travolta's "official" screen debut came in a supporting role in *Carrie* (pictured with Nancy Allen).

Seven

Disco Dreamboat

Saturday Night Fever 1977

Paramount Pictures. Director: John Badham. Producer: Robert
Stigwood. Screenplay: Norman Wexler, based on a *New York* magazine
article by Nik Cohn. Cinematographer: Ralf D. Bode. Music: Barry,
Robin, and Maurice Gibb, and David Shire. Editor: David Rawlins.
CAST: John Travolta *(Tony Manero)*, Karen Lynn Gorney *(Stephanie)*,
Barry Miller *(Bobby C.)*, Joseph Cali *(Joey)*, Paul Pape *(Double J.)*, Donna
Pescow *(Annette)*, Bruce Ornstein *(Gus)*, Julie Bovasso *(Flo)*, Martin
Shakar *(Frank Jr.)*, Sam J. Coppola *(Fusco)*, Nina Hansen *(Grandmother)*,
Lisa Peluso *(Linda)* Denny Dillon *(Doreen)*, Fran Drescher *(Connie)*,
Robert Costanza [Costanzo] *(Paint Store Customer)*, Ann Travolta *(Pizza
Girl)*, Helen Travolta *(Lady in Paint Store)*.
119 minutes. Rated: R (Alternate version: 108 minutes. Rated: PG).

John Travolta was not destined to be eternally identified as Vinnie
Barbarino. He signed a three-picture deal with producer Robert
Stigwood and became a major movie star with his first film under
the contract: *Saturday Night Fever*, as much an event as a motion
picture in that it was to transcend its own astounding popularity
by serving to define the pop culture of a generation. Travolta's
Tony Manero, disco hunk supreme, is a variation of Vinnie
Barbarino as a tough but likable Italian-American street kid from
Brooklyn. However, while Barbarino functioned mainly as a comical
character, there is a serious edge to Manero. While Barbarino was part
of an ensemble, Manero is the focus of the story. Whenever he is on-
screen, all eyes are diverted to him.

It was the combination of Travolta's poster-boy good looks and
working-class attitude which further attracted (predominantly female)
moviegoers to him, and his slick dance floor moves to the finger-pop-
ping beat of the Bee Gees aided immeasurably in making disco *the* pop
craze of the era. As *Newsweek* magazine noted as 1977 came to a close,
"Not even Sweathog freaks will be prepared for the new Travolta. His
presence is electric, his dancing spectacular. In *Fever*, Travolta makes a

Travolta, at the time of his *Saturday Night Fever* ascendence.

rare leap for a stereotyped TV actor—and lands as a real movie star." Immediately upon its release, *Saturday Night Fever* became a runaway hit. During its first sixteen-plus weeks in movie houses, it grossed over $81 million—and it needed to earn only one-eleventh of that figure to turn a profit.

In retrospect, Travolta's Tony Manero is one of the icons of 1970s pop culture. He is as much a model of the period as Valentino and Clara Bow reflect the innocent romanticism and gusto of the 1920s, Henry Fonda's Tom Joad mirrors the despair of the Depression, Bogart in a trenchcoat symbolizes the shadowy uncertainty of the dawn of the atomic age, or Dustin Hoffman's Graduate and Dennis Hopper's and Peter Fonda's Easy Riders reflect the Baby Boomer alienation of the late 1960s. In *Mr. Holland's Opus*, a 1995 feature which opens in 1965 and charts thirty years in the life of a high school music teacher, images of famous personalities and events are used to mark the passage of time.

Manero on the make: Travolta's Tony Manero admires Stephanie (Karen Lynn Gorney), and playfully teases her.

They include Nixon and Agnew, Gerald Ford stumbling as he exits an airplane, John Lennon "imagining" a world at peace, John Lennon assassinated—and, appropriately, John Travolta in *Saturday Night Fever*.

The origins of Tony Manero as a character actually may be linked to the bad boy teen icons of the 1950s: James Dean and his Actors Studio angst in *Rebel Without a Cause*, Marlon Brando astride a motorcycle in *The Wild One*, and the hip-swiveling Elvis of *Jailhouse Rock* and *King Creole*. All oozed sexuality while setting the juices flowing in teenage girls, whose male counterparts became determined to duplicate their aura of hipness. A new kind of movie star was on the horizon: the antihero. He may have been consistently and brilliantly played by John Garfield starting in the late 1930s, but he did not become a staple on movie screens until the 1950s.

Add to the formula the advent of rock 'n' roll. *Blackboard Jungle*, a story of inner-city juvenile delinquent high schoolers who made the Bowery Boys seem like babes in the woods, is the first film to feature rock music on the soundtrack: Bill Haley and His Comets' "Rock Around the Clock," heard over the opening credits. Two decades later, there was a new kind of music: disco, yet another phase in the evolution of rock 'n' roll, to be sure, but an altogether fresh sound with an infectious and highly danceable beat. In 1978, disco and Tony Manero, its sexiest practitioner, were on the cutting edge. *Saturday Night Fever* was to gross over $400 million worldwide, with the film's soundtrack album selling like icy glasses of lemonade on a sweltering summer day.

The film is based on "Tribal Rites of the New Saturday Night," an article by Nik Cohn in the June 1976 issue of *New York* magazine. In it, Cohn chronicles the story of "Vincent," a third-generation Italian-American Brooklynite who electrifies the dance floor at 2001 Odyssey, a popular neighborhood disco.

Travolta's star is born the instant he appears on screen. With the Bee Gees' "Stayin' Alive" on the soundtrack, he is captured in different camera angles as he strides down a street with a paint can in his hand, his weight resting in his hips. He eyes every attractive girl he passes, and even tries to pick one up. This is the macho Tony Manero, the Tony who is beloved by his buddies and coveted by all the neighborhood girls, beauty and bimbo alike. At the same time, he might as well be a Martian to his elders, as he is hassled by his out-of-work father (because he is young and sexy, and has no responsibilities) and religion-obsessed mother (because he has not chosen to enter the priesthood, like his older brother).

Tony has spent his nineteen years in his Bay Ridge neighborhood. By day, he works as a clerk in a paint store. He has no education. He has no prospects. Twenty years into the future, you expect him to still be toiling among the paint cans, struggling to support a wife and several half-grown bambinos, acting out his own suppressed feeling of failure by hassling his own children. Tony, as many his age, only wishes to live in the present. His boss offers him some sage advice: "No, Tony. You can't fuck the future. The future fucks you."

From nine-to-five, Tony may be just another neighborhood minimum wage slave. But at night, he comes alive. First he goes through the ritual of preparing himself for the evening. With the Bee Gees' "Night

Fever" on the soundtrack, he carefully blow-dries and combs his hair, and poses in front of a mirror garbed in nothing but his black bikini underwear. Then he dresses up in his polyester togs. He joins his friends, and they head for 2001 Odyssey, the same disco which was the center-piece of Nik Cohn's article, where Tony reigns as the prettiest boy and best dancer. Tony's sense of identity is inseparable from the 2001 Odyssey dance floor, where his slick, sexy moves to "dancin' yeah" lyrics and a pulsating disco beat have earned him respect.

Had he lived in the 1950s, Tony's cultural icons would have been Marlon Brando and James Dean; no Italian-American movie stars were their equivalent. While he never could approach the popularity of the real-life pop culture heroes whose posters adorn his bedroom walls (Sylvester Stallone as *Rocky*, Al Pacino as *Serpico*), at 2001 Odyssey, Tony Manero is the star.

The club's dance floor is transparent and lit from underneath. The lights also flash, which makes for a visually dazzling setting as Tony strides out to dance. By far, these sequences, scattered throughout *Saturday Night Fever*, are the film's highlights. They are the ones which helped to solidify Travolta's stardom.

While Tony Manero is no social outcast as is James Dean's Jim Stark in *Rebel Without a Cause*, both characters are sensitive. Beneath his macho exterior, Tony is, after all, a dancer. He is misunderstood by, and alienated from, his family. In particular, his father is not an authority fig-ure who commands respect.

In essence, *Saturday Night Fever* is a coming-of-age story as Tony slowly realizes that the boundaries of the future stretch beyond Bay Ridge. His brother decides to leave the priesthood, and fulfill his own destiny rather than fashion his life solely to please his mother; Tony sees that he, too, can make independent choices. He is attracted to the beau-tiful Stephanie (Karen Lynn Gorney), whom he first convinces to be his partner in a dance contest at 2001 Odyssey and with whom he develops a complex relationship. While doing so, he sees that "girls" are more

than just receptacles for quick sex. At the film's close, Tony and Stephanie solidify what is described as a "friendship"—an involvement with a woman which the Tony Manero seen at the beginning of the film could never, ever be capable of having.

In the end, *Saturday Night Fever*—despite its sex scenes, hard language, and R rating—is a variation of the classic, studio-produced movie musical about the talented unknown who must find himself before he can find success. At the finale, there is the hint that the road which Tony will take will lead him to Broadway: a promise which would be fulfilled in *Staying Alive*, the film's sequel.

But *Saturday Night Fever* is the story of Tony Manero in Brooklyn. As such, the Borough of Churches is practically a character in the film, with Tony (like Vinnie Barbarino before him) becoming as much of a geographical stereotype as William Bendix had been to an earlier generation. Back in the 1940s, the likably chubby Bendix appeared in numerous films playing "woiking" class joes from Flatbush who lived on "toidy-toid-an-toid" and were obsessed with everything Brooklyn. Manero is very much the stereotypical Brooklyn boy, and so it is appropriate, then, that *Saturday Night Fever* opens with a shot of the Brooklyn Bridge.

However, in the film, Brooklyn is shown to be a place from

Tony contemplates his life choices. Should he follow in the footsteps of his older brother and join the priesthood? Similarly, his adolescent angst, and his attempt to find an identity separate and distinct from his parents, mirrors the plight of James Dean's Jim Stark in *Rebel Without a Cause*.

Tony, a la Vinnie Barbarino, expresses himself with his hands. But in *Saturday Night Fever*, he also gets to use his fists.

which to escape. In recent years, Brooklyn-on-screen is more often the habitat of Latino or African-American drug dealers (as depicted in *Ghost* and *Clockers*, among other films) or the setting for volatile ethnic confrontation (most memorably, in *Do the Right Thing*). While the Brooklyn characters in *Saturday Night Fever* are not out-and-out lowlifes, they still are unattractive. Tony's parents are ethnic neurotics. His pals are bonded by a ganglike mentality. They aimlessly rumble with "spics"—in Brooklyn, Italians dump on "spics" while "spics" dump on Italians— and show off by performing foolhardy, potentially dangerous acrobatics on the Verrazano Bridge. Annette, the neighborhood girl who covets Tony the most, is willing to have sex with him so that she may get pregnant—and then he will have to marry her. Finally, his buddies at 2001 would, out of favoritism, award him and Stephanie first prize in the dance contest, even though Tony knows that a Puerto Rican duo is more deserving of the honor. This, as much as anything else, rattles the sense of values that has been lying dormant within him, obscured by his macho façade.

Stephanie, meanwhile, adores Manhattan, the borough that is the promised land, the glitzy alternative to blue-collar Brooklyn. To her

Travolta on the *Saturday Night Fever* set with director John Badham (right).

way of thinking, all the interesting and creative people live and work across the Brooklyn Bridge. Her wish is to shut the door on Bay Ridge, and transport herself to a Manhattan Tower. However, while you can take the girl out of Brooklyn, you cannot take Brooklyn out of the girl. Stephanie's accent is strictly Brooklynese, and she is just as unsophisticated as Tony as she tells him how urbane Manhattan working women shop at "Bonwit-Taylor." She may be a class above the other Bay Ridge females, but in Manhattan she is little more than a rough-around-the-edges gofer at a talent agency. The ugly side of Manhattan corporate life is revealed when Stephanie admits to Tony that she has had to sleep with one of her superiors just to keep her job. "He's been helping me," is her excuse.

Another prominent component of *Saturday Night Fever* is the Bee Gees' pulsating disco score. The power of the music is a constant in the film, not just when Travolta is gyrating on the dance floor but when he is strutting down the street or preparing for a night at 2001 Odyssey. While Travolta won an Academy Award nomination for playing Tony Manero—he had earlier been cited as the year's Best Actor by the National Board of Review—one of the Oscar scandals was that the Bee

Tony converses with Bobby C. (Barry Miller), who is destined to fall to his death from the Verrazano Bridge. Bobby C. is *Saturday Night Fever's* equivalent of Sal Mineo's Plato character in *Rebel Without a Cause*: younger than the hero, and fated to die. In *Rebel*, Mineo is shot to death by the police.

Gees were aced out of nominations for Best Original Score and individual song. Their music was disqualified by the Academy because it had not been written specifically for the film.

In the Original Score category, their effort surely might have replaced as a nominee the lilting music from *Mohammad–Messenger of God*. In the Best Song competition, the nominees were equally lackluster: "The Slipper and the Rose," "Candle on the Water," "Someone's Waiting for You," "Nobody Does It Better" (easily the best of the lot), and the goopy "You Light Up My Life," the eventual winner. But this slight did nothing to diminish the Bee Gees' popularity. In 1979, they played concerts across America in what *People* magazine described as "the hottest tour since the Beatles." When they played Houston, the already delighted crowd was in for a special surprise: a bearded Travolta (who was in the area filming *Urban Cowboy*) joined them onstage where he recreated some of his *Saturday Night Fever* dance moves.

The *Saturday Night Fever* script, penned by Norman Wexler, is laced with street language and profanity—while ranking someone out, Tony and his buddies employ phrases far more graphic than "Up your nose with a rubber hose"—and the film originally was R-rated. To make it accessible to teenyboppers, Paramount ordered an alternate version. Eleven minutes of footage were deleted, with scenes and dialogue completely changed or eliminated. The adjusted version was rated PG.

None of *Saturday Night Fever*'s other principal actors were to enjoy a fame in any way approaching that of Travolta. Most noticeably, Karen Lynn Gorney was to win no other important movie roles. Before *Saturday Night Fever*, she had played Tara Martin on *All My Children*; afterwards, she returned to the show for several years. Meanwhile, two of the film's bit players have had successful careers. Connie, the neighborhood girl who appears in one scene and asks Tony if he is as good in bed as he is on the dance floor, is played by young Fran Drescher, light years away from *The Nanny*. Robert Costanzo (billed as "Costanza"), cast as one of Tony's paint store customers, became a noted character actor. He is especially adept at playing gangsters, as he did on several episodes of *NYPD Blue*. If you do not recognize his name, you certainly will know his face.

2001 Odyssey, the Brooklyn disco, profited greatly from its exposure in *Saturday Night Fever*. In an article titled "Brooklyn: Disco Capital of the Nation," published in 1978 in the inaugural issue of *Brooklyn* magazine, 2001 Odyssey was described as "probably the second most famous disco in the world"—after Manhattan's Studio 54. *Saturday Night Fever* movie posters were "practically wallpapered to the club." Tourists from as far away as France and Belgium, let alone Manhattan and Staten Island, were trekking there to shake their booties on the same floor as Travolta.

Saturday Night Fever: Memorable Lines

Tony to his father, who has just slapped him at the dinner table: "I work on my hair a long time, and you hit it. He hits my hair."

Deejay at the 2001 Odyssey: "I like that polyester look, man. Turn yourself in, baby."

Tony to his parents, as he arrives home late one night: "What is this? I walk in, you don't got no criticism of me?"

Tony's father, to Tony: "You know what four dollars buys today? It don't even buy three dollars."

Girl to Tony, on the 2001 Odyssey dance floor: "Kiss me. Kiss me." He kisses her. "Oooooh, I just kissed Al Pacino."

Tony to Annette, while having sex: "You fixed? Huh? You fixed? . . . What you got? The I.O.U.? That thing?"

Stephanie, telling Tony about Laurence Olivier: "He's the greatest actor in the whole world. . . . He's the English actor. The one on television who does all those Polaroid commercials." Tony to Stephanie: "Do you think that you could get a camera from him, like at a discount?"

Stephanie to Tony: "You're a cliché. You're nowhere. On your way to no place."

Frank Jr., Tony's older brother, to Tony: "You know, your dancing is really marvelous. It's exciting. . . . They can't keep their eyes off you."

Frank Jr. to Tony, later on: "What about you? Are you gonna do something with your dancing, Tony? . . . . The only way you're gonna survive is to do what you think is right. Not what *they* keep trying to jam you into. You let them do that and you're gonna end up nothing but miserable."

Eight

Parodies and Homages

everal of Travolta's scenes in *Saturday Night Fever*—notably the opening one and his dance floor solos—are part of cinema folklore. They are so instantly identifiable that they have become fodder for parody in other films.

Easily the funniest *Saturday Night Fever* takeoff came in 1980, in *Airplane!*, Jim Abrahams and David and Jerry Zucker's spoof of *Airport*-style disaster films. Robert Hays stars as Ted Striker, pilot-turned-cab driver who has been unable to come near an airplane since "the war." He loves Elaine (Julie Hagerty), a stewardess who has rejected him because of his hang-up. In order to pursue her, he purchases a ticket on her Los Angeles-to-Chicago flight.

Ted reminisces to a fellow passenger about his first meeting with Elaine. "It was during the war," he says. "I was in the air force, stationed in Drambuie, off the Barbary Coast." His favored hang-out was a sleazy, rough-and-tumble bar, "the seediest dive on the wharf, populated with every reject and cutthroat from Bombay to Calcutta"—and a universe away from 2001 Odyssey.

He continues, "The mood in the place was downright ugly. You couldn't walk in there unless you knew how to use your fists. You could count on a fight breaking out almost every night." At this juncture, two girls in Scout uniforms begin a knockdown, chair-busting brawl. One has her head slammed into a jukebox, at which point the Bee Gees' "Stayin' Alive" comes on the soundtrack and the hard dames and knife-wielding old salts, who look like extras from a pirate movie, come alive and begin boogying to the music.

Ted remains at the bar, with drink in hand, until he spies Elaine across the dance floor. He is "captivated" and "entranced" by her. After throwing off his cap, he approaches her. They stare into each other's eyes. He whips off his air force jacket and, voila, he becomes a John Travolta/Tony Manero clone, garbed in white pants, white vest, and black polyester shirt. He strikes a Manero-esque pose, and he and Elaine begin to dance. Soon they are acrobatically tossing and swinging each other. Ted then takes to the floor in a solo, with Hays deftly and hilariously parodying Travolta's 2001 Odyssey moves in a manner which gravity does not allow.

"We laughed. We talked. We danced. I didn't want it to end," Ted concludes. He is oblivious to the fact that the passenger to whom he has been relating this story has hanged herself from boredom.

The woman's reaction is meant to parody the increasing cries of "disco is dead" being heard in 1980. The same is true later on in the film, in the sequence in which the airplane flies perilously low over the Chicago skyline. Just as a radio disc jockey announces "WZAZ in Chicago, where disco lives forever," the plane knocks down the station's antenna, thus silencing the deejay.

Travolta and *Saturday Night Fever* have, over the years, remained sharp as a celluloid reference point. *Cocoon*, a 1985 fantasy, is set in a Florida retirement community where the lives of three seniors (Don Ameche, Hume Cronyn, and Wilford Brimley) revolve around doctors' visits and impending death. After swimming in a pool amid some mysterious pods which have been placed there by aliens, they regain their youthful spunk. Suddenly, they feel "great" and "tremendous," and even have "boners." One evening, they take their women to a disco. As Art Selwyn (Ameche) begins slow-dancing with Bess McCarthy (Gwen Verdon) amid the twentysomething disco-denizens, he is met with friendly teases of "grandpa" and "look at the old folks." Selwyn one-ups them by striking a Travoltaesque pose and executing a snazzy breakdance solo that is reminiscent of Tony Manero's 2001 Odyssey acrobatics. It is highlighted by his spinning himself across the floor, and ends with him stretching his arm out above his head in triumph, à la Travolta. All that is missing from the scene is "Stayin' Alive" on the soundtrack.

At the other end of the age scale, in *Look Who's Talking*, Travolta's 1989 comedy, Mikey the toddler (voiced on the soundtrack by Bruce Willis) becomes a junior Tony Manero. As he is being walked in his stroller, "Stayin' Alive" comes on the soundtrack. Mikey passes other babies—girl babies—and Willis's voice converses with them and makes comments about them.

Fifteen years after *Airplane!*, Travolta and Tony Manero are lampooned in *Virtuosity*, an unpleasant, corpse-littered thriller. Denzel Washington plays a former cop, now a convict, who is dispatched to track down Sid 6.7 (Russell Crowe), a virtual-reality–created maniac who has escaped from cyberspace and set out on a murderous rampage.

Several characters discuss his status. One, a criminal psychologist (Kelly Lynch), explains, "Sid 6.7 isn't bound by programming anymore. In the real world, he's free of any behavioral limits he might have had in virtual reality."

Responds a colleague, "He's evolving. My god, he's evolving."

Adds another, "Into what?"

Cut to a nattily-dressed Sid 6.7, strutting through a mall. "Stayin' Alive" fills the soundtrack. Sid 6.7 is shot from similar camera angles as Tony Manero at the opening of *Saturday Night Fever*.

The effect at first seems farcical. Of all the human beings in the world to emulate, Sid 6.7 is evolving into—Tony Manero! However, just before, Sid 6.7 had terrorized the patrons of a contemporary disco, one with futuristic lights and oversized video monitors. He had grabbed attention at the disco, as Tony had owned 2001 Odyssey, so in his mind he has earned the right to strut.

Finally, in 1995's *Grumpier Old Men*, after successfully romancing Maria Ragetti (a still-ravishing Sophia Loren), old fart Max Goldman (Walter Matthau) does some slick dance steps to "Stayin' Alive."

Travolta himself willingly has lampooned *Saturday Night Fever*. In 1994, the *Saturday Night Live* show he guest-hosted opens with the camera tracking his feet as he strides down a corridor. He is accompanied by the beat of "Stayin' Alive," and he soon addresses a pretty female NBC page. But his attention towards her is not sexual, as one might expect from Tony Manero. "Hi. Could you tell me where the bathroom is?" he asks, and the skit continues on in a similar vein.

While disco and polyester now seem like artifacts of a distant American past, young John Travolta and his celluloid stardom will forever be linked to that era—not only in America but the world over. You've heard of *The Man With Bogart's Face. Garbo Talks. Fred and Ginger. Come Back to the 5 & Dime, Jimmy Dean, Jimmy Dean.* Add to the list *Travolta and Me*—original title: *Travolta et moi*— a 1993 French-language feature directed by Patricia Mazuy. The 68-minute-long film is one of a ten-part series, titled *All the Boys and Girls of Their Time* and produced for French television. It is set in the late 1970s, when Travolta, *Saturday Night Fever*, and disco music were the rage.

Travolta and Me tells the story of Nicolas (Julien Gerin), a seventeen-year-old who reads Nietzche and Rimbaud, and bets that he can seduce any girl. He sets his sights on sixteen-year-old Christine (Leslie Azzoulai), who is consumed by Travolta—and who misconstrues Nicolas's attention, thinking he is interested in romance rather than sex.

New York Times critic Stephen Holden called *Travolta and Me* "a story of adolescent passion run amok . . . [which] captures the eruptions and vulnerability of adolescence with an almost embarrassing acuity"— a description that is just as fitting for *Saturday Night Fever*.

Finally, as with countless hit movies, *Saturday Night Fever* was the model for several television series (albeit unsuccessful ones). *Joe and Valerie*, for example, ran on NBC between April and May 1978, and briefly reappeared in January 1979. It starred Paul Regina as blue-collar Brooklynite Joe Pizo and Char Fontane as Valerie, his disco-dancing partner and betrothed. Robert Costanzo played Vince Pizo, Joe's widowed plumber father.

Then there was *Makin' It*, which ran on ABC between February and March 1979. The setting may have been Passaic, New Jersey, rather than Brooklyn, but even a dolt would not miss the similarity to *Saturday Night Fever*. The show's title was a synonym for *Stayin' Alive*. Tony

Manucci (rather than Manero), played by Greg Antonacci, brother of college student Billy (David Naughton), was the hottest dancer at the Inferno, Passaic's most popular disco.

Playing the Manucci brothers' mother, in a clever bit of casting, was none other than Ellen Travolta, John's big sister!

Nine

Travolta the Fashion Plate

In *Saturday Night Fever*, there is a special focus on Tony as he dresses up, and beautifies himself, for his evening at 2001 Odyssey. This emphasis on male attire, and the ritual of a man dressing up, was—and is—a rarity in films.

Travolta was not the first fashion-oriented male on screen: a top hat and tails were key elements of Fred Astaire's on-screen personality. In *Swing Time*, Astaire plays John "Lucky" Garnett, a dancer-gambler who, as the film opens, is shown dressing for his wedding in the company of his fellow performers. Lamenting to Garnett, his sidekick (Victor Moore) says that he hates "to see you leave show business." So one of the dancers draws cuffs on some trousers pictured in a magazine. Then all of them compare Garnett's pants to the photo, declaring, "Last year's trousers. No cuffs!" How can Garnett wed while garbed in out-of-style clothes? He allows the pants to be brought to a tailor, which leads to his being late for his nuptials—the act which sets the plot in motion.

In *Top Hat*—a title which directly refers to male fashion—Astaire's character and his pal (Edward Everett Horton) are shown debating what constitutes proper formal attire. The latter notes that his valet "insists that a square tie is the only possible tie that can be worn with evening clothes . . . I prefer the butterfly." And of course, in the title song, Astaire sings of dressing up in a top hat, white tie, and tails.

Such an emphasis on fashion might be considered unmasculine. But Astaire could be linked to clothes because he was so suave and likable. His sexual chemistry while dancing with Ginger Rogers in both these films was unmistakable. Travolta, too, posed no threat to heterosexual males. Tony Manero's narcissism as he dressed up was designed to make him attractive to women. His intention was to seduce Stephanie, not her brother. After watching him make himself up for his evening at 2001 Odyssey, male viewers did not consider him sissified. Rather, they wanted to imitate him.

Such also was the case with *American Gigolo*, released three years

(Opposite) In *Saturday Night Fever* and its sequel, *Staying Alive*, there is a special emphasis on the manner in which Tony Manero is dressed. In the latter, no generic, off-the-rack leather jacket will do for Tony, even though his character is that of a struggling dancer.

after *Saturday Night Fever*. While the fashion sense in *Gigolo* is diametrically opposed to that in *Fever*, the latter was nevertheless influenced by the former. In *American Gigolo*, Richard Gere plays a style-conscious, Giorgio Armani–clad male prostitute—a role originally intended for Travolta! As Tony Manero is shown dressing himself for the evening, Gere's Julian also carefully selects his wardrobe from his closet, with rock music on the soundtrack.

American Gigolo, as *Saturday Night Fever* and *Urban Cowboy* (which featured Travolta in western shirts and hats, Levi's, and boots), was to influence male fashion trends. And, arguably, the depiction of Julian carefully beautifying himself might not have been possible without the prior audience acceptance of Tony Manero doing the same.

Ten

That's Dancing! . . . That's Travolta

In 1985, *That's Dancing!*, a compilation film in the *That's Entertainment* mode, came to movie theaters. It featured narration by Mikhail Baryshnikov, Ray Bolger, Sammy Davis Jr., Gene Kelly, and Liza Minnelli, and clips spotlighting all of the great names associated with dance on screen.

Choreographer Busby Berkeley is described as having begun "to take the camera where it had never been. . . . His overhead shots became his trademark." Ruby Keeler is "the first great dancing star of the 1930s," and Fred Astaire is "style, elegance, charm, and class personified"; when Astaire was paired with Ginger Rogers, dance became an expression of "romantic love." Bill "Bojangles" Robinson is "an idol, an inspiration to several generations of dancers. His control and balance were legendary." Eleanor Powell is "the very best" of "all the dancing ladies of the 1930s." The Nicholas Brothers are "the most successful specialty team in movie history," while Ray Bolger "could do it all." The 1940s and 1950s were "the golden years of the movie musical," with MGM having in its stable "the number-one dancer, and the number-one dancer, Fred Astaire and Gene Kelly."

In *That's Dancing!*, John Travolta is given equal time with these legends. Kelly in fact narrates the final portion of the film, which is devoted to dance in contemporary motion pictures. The first hoofer he introduces—followed by those from *Fame*, uncredited stand-in dancer Marine Jahan in *Flashdance*, and Michael Jackson in the music video of *Beat It*—is Travolta.

"The music of the eighties has had a profound influence on movie dancing. . . ," Kelly observes, adding that ". . . disco dancing was never more graphically presented than in *Saturday Night Fever*. The music of the Bee Gees highlighted the most talked-about element in the movie: the spectacular dancing of John Travolta." Next came a clip of Travolta and his flashy moves on the 2001 Odyssey dance floor.

Travolta on the 2001 Odyssey dance floor.

Writer Norma McLain Stoop, an observer on the set of *Staying Alive*, the *Saturday Night Fever* sequel, observed: "Anyone who sees Travolta dance the dramatic production number [at the film's finale] will sense that fire and urgency. They may also sense, as I did while watching the number being filmed, Travolta's consuming desire to perfect

every movement of that limber body he worked so hard to get into dancing shape.

"He's tremendously aware of the perpetuation of the continuity of the American film dancing tradition, with its very special vitality."

In the compilation documentary *That's Dancing!*, Travolta the dancer is cited along with such legendary celluloid hoofers as Bill "Bojangles" Robinson and Gene Kelly *(above)*.

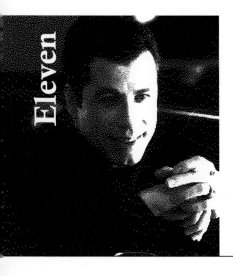

Travolta Is the Word

Grease 1978

Paramount Pictures. Director: Randal Kleiser. Producers: Robert
Stigwood and Allan Carr. Screenplay: Bronte Woodard. Adaptation:
Allan Carr, based on the original musical by Jim Jacobs and Warren
Casey. Cinematographer: Bill Butler. Music Supervisor: Bill Oakes.
Grease music and lyrics: Barry Gibb. Dances and musical sequences
staged and choreographed by Patricia Birch. Editor: John F. Burnett.
CAST: John Travolta *(Danny)*, Olivia Newton-John *(Sandy)*, Stockard
Channing *(Rizzo)*, Jeff Conaway *(Kenickie)*, Barry Pearl *(Doody)*, Michael
Tucci *(Sonny)*, Kelly Ward *(Putzie)*, Didi Conn *(Frenchy)*, Jamie Donnelly
(Jan), Dinah Manoff *(Marty)*, Susan Buckner *(Patty Simcox)*, Eddie
Deezen *(Eugene)*, Lorenzo Lamas *(Tom Chisum)*, Dennis Stewart *(Leo)*,
Annette Charles *(Cha Cha)*, Dick Patterson *(Mr. Rudie)*, Fannie Flagg
(Nurse Wilkin), Ellen Travolta *(Waitress)*, Eve Arden *(Principal McGee)*,
Frankie Avalon *(Teen Angel)*, Joan Blondell *(Vi)*, Edd Byrnes *(Vince
Fontaine)*, Sid Caesar *(Coach Calhoun)*, Alice Ghostley *(Mrs. Murdock)*,
Dody Goodman *(Blanche)*, Sha-Na-Na *(Johnny Casino and the Gamblers)*.
110 minutes. Rated: PG.

Travolta's successful follow-up to *Saturday Night Fever* was the
musical *Grease*, a nostalgic ode to 1950s greaser/doo-wop teen
culture. Here, he has another letter-perfect screen role: Danny
Zuko, a character who, essentially, is a de-Brooklynized variation of Vinnie Barbarino and Tony Manero. Travolta agreed to
do the film because, as he explained in 1978, "There aren't
that many musicals around to do—who knows when I'll ever
do another?—and I thought it a good move for me. Brando did
a musical, *Guys and Dolls*, very early in his career."

Steve Krantz, the former partner of animator Ralph Bakshi and
husband of best-selling novelist Judith Krantz, initially owned the movie
rights to *Grease*, and he had wanted to produce it as a feature-length cartoon. He was unable to finance the project, and the rights eventually
were picked up by Allan Carr, who became the film's coproducer.

Grease originally was to be shot before *Saturday Night Fever*, and

Carr first pictured Henry "Fonzie" Winkler as Danny. Happily for Travolta, Winkler nixed the role. The result for the young superstar was an even bigger success, as *Grease* became the number-one box-office attraction of 1978; it eventually earned worldwide grosses of over $450 million, making it the top moneymaking movie musical in history. Its soundtrack album was as much of a hot-seller as the one for the earlier film. Indeed, both are among the most popular albums in history, with *Saturday Night Fever* selling 35 million copies worldwide and *Grease* checking in at 24 million copies sold.

In *Grease*, Travolta isn't really called upon to act. Instead, he dances. He sings. He strikes "yo, dude" poses. His hair is strictly pre-army Elvis: slick, piled high and, of course, gloriously greasy. He is oh, so cool as a cigarette dangles from his lips. He doesn't so much walk as saunter, and bop. He never, ever would get soft on a girl.

Travolta's Danny Zuko projects attitude the way Elvis did in

Danny's gang.

Jailhouse Rock, or Brando in *The Wild One*, or James Dean in *Rebel Without a Cause*. But *Grease* is a musical-comedy that is steeped in sweet nostalgia for a simpler, more idealized age—a pre-Kennedy assassination, pre–Vietnam War era in which high school girls were proud to be dating marines, and a teen's biggest problem was pimples. For all intents and purposes, Danny's sunglasses—or "shades," as he would say—were rose-colored. You won't find him mouthing off at teachers or fighting with a drawn switchblade in the classroom (as is the case in *Blackboard Jungle*). When he drag-races, it is anticlimatic rather than an emotional high-point of the story (as is the case in *Rebel Without a Cause*).

Like Henry Winkler's Fonzie on *Happy Days* (and decidedly unlike the characters upon which they are modeled), Danny is no angst-ridden or ill-fated juvenile delinquent. Instead, he stars on the dance floor during the telecast of an *American Bandstand*–like show. After Travolta's smashing success dancing in *Saturday Night Fever*, there was no way that he could have avoided dancing in *Grease*. Indeed, throughout his career, directors and scriptwriters have managed to place Travolta on dance floors, even if only for the briefest of interludes.

One would expect Danny to be attracted to the sluttish Rizzo (Stockard Channing), the kind of girl who would shrug her shoulders before going all the way in the back seat of a jalopy. However, Danny and blond, virginal Sandy (Olivia Newton-John) have just enjoyed an idyllic summer romance. As the school year begins, Sandy is set to return to her native Australia. Danny, as he starts his senior year at Rydell High School, dons the black leather motorcycle jacket he had foregone during his interlude with Sandy and resumes his identity as one of the T-Birds, a gang of greasers and practical jokers. However, Sandy's plans have been altered and, to Danny's surprise, he finds that she has enrolled at Rydell. Danny and Sandy spend the rest of the film negotiating their relationship amid a climate of pep rallies, malt shops, and drive-in movies.

Grease serves as a celebration of tacky 1950s teen culture: a culture which glorifies such Grade Z horror/sci-fi films as *Attack of the 50-Foot Woman, Teen-age Caveman, I Was a Teen-age Werewolf,* and *Queen of Outer Space,* as well as low-budget teen-angst features like *Hot Rod Rumble, Speed Crazy, Reform School Girl, Joy Ride,* and *The Cool and the Crazy.* As a mixture of music and romantic soap opera, it is linked to some of the first rock 'n' roll movies: *Rock, Rock, Rock, Rock Around the Clock, Mr. Rock and Roll, Jamboree,* and *Go, Johnny, Go!*—films that were not very good back in the 1950s, but were controversial in that they featured white, middle-class teens enjoying black performers and music. Indeed, *Grease* succeeds as a first-rate spoof of films like *Rock, Rock, Rock* and *Rock Around the Clock,* along with the Frankie Avalon/Annette Funicello *Beach Party/Beach Blanket Bingo* surf-and-sand epics of the early-to-mid-1960s.

The screenplay of *Grease* is crammed with pop cultural references, such as Sandra Dee, Troy Donahue, Annette—back in the late 1950s, the "Funicello" was redundant—and Debbie Reynolds's *Tammy.* The cast is studded with 1950s television stars and teen idols, including Frankie Avalon (looking great as he appears in a fantasy sequence in which he sings the satirical ballad "Beauty School Dropout"), Edd "Kookie" Byrnes (as a Dick Clark–like emcee), Eve Arden (as a Rydell

Rydell High Coach Calhoun (Sid Caesar) attempts to explain the finer points of athletics to Danny.

authority figure whose name is not Miss Brooks, and who spouts such lines as "If you can't be an athlete, be an athletic supporter"), and Sid Caesar (as the Rydell athletic coach). There even is a link to the Warner Bros. Busby Berkeley musicals of the 1930s, with the appearance of Joan Blondell—the star of *Gold Diggers of 1933*, *Footlight Parade*, and *Dames*—cast as a waitress.

In 1982, a *Grease* sequel was released, but without Travolta and Newton-John. Original cast members Eve Arden, Sid Caesar, Didi Conn, and Dody Goodman all appeared, along with Maxwell Caulfield, Lorna Luft, Adrian Zmed, Tab Hunter, Connie Stevens, and a young Michelle Pfeiffer. This time around, "grease" was no longer the word. *Grease 2* took in a lackluster $6.5 million at the box office.

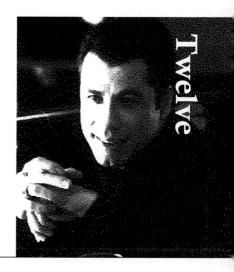

"Next to This Film, *Grease* Looks Like *Citizen Kane*"

Moment by Moment 1978

Universal Pictures. Director-Screenplay: Jane Wagner. Producer: Robert Stigwood. Cinematographer: Philip Lathrop. Music: Lee Holdridge. Editor: John F. Burnett. CAST: Lily Tomlin *(Trisha)*, John Travolta *(Strip)*, Andra Akers *(Naomi)*, Bert Kramer *(Stu)*, Shelley R. Bonus *(Peg)*, Debra Feuer *(Stacie)*, James Luisi *(Dan Santini)*. 105 minutes. Rated: R.

Travolta's popularity in *Saturday Night Fever* and *Grease* derives from the fact that his characters are attractive. Whatever their flaws, they are in charge. They are aggressive. They exude machismo. All of the action centers around them.

Yet as he attained stardom, Travolta expressed a desire to take roles that would play against his established persona. While on hiatus from *Welcome Back, Kotter*, he toured in *Bus Stop* because, as he explained in 1978, "it was a chance to fight that typing thing, play a western dude instead of all these urban types."

One year after *Saturday Night Fever*, and the same year as *Grease*, he appeared opposite Lily Tomlin in *Moment by Moment*—and Travolta was not kidding when he described his character as "a *completely* different guy than anything I've played so far." He was cast as Strip, a street kid and drifter who becomes the romantic object of Trisha (Tomlin), a well-heeled Malibu housewife/older woman. Strip is no chip-on-his-shoulder punk, à la Vinnie Barbarino/Tony Manero/Danny Zuko. He puts forth such un-macho qualities as sensitivity, submissiveness, defenselessness. He is feminizied, in that his character is the one who needs to be loved, while Tomlin's is the one who is interested in sex. "Look," he tells her, "when you're ready to admit you love me, you can have me—and not until." At another point, Strip even breaks out in tears.

There are, of course, love scenes in *Moment by Moment*. In them, in order to symbolize the dominance of Trisha, Tomlin is strategically placed on top of Travolta.

But good intentions do not necessarily make good movies. *Moment by Moment* is a well-meaning but ultimately superficial attempt at a feminist statement. It also is, by anyone's standards, a dreadful film, which earned scathing, career-wrecking reviews:

> . . . this year's California problem picture. . . . It's very difficult to understand what Miss Tomlin and Jane Wagner, who wrote and directed the film, wanted to do in *Moment by Moment*. As romantic drama it's pretty tepid. That the two stars look enough alike to be brother and sister is no help. . . . One has the impression that these two lovers would prefer to be doing something else.
>
> —VINCENT CANBY, *NEW YORK TIMES*

> . . . A fizzle . . . it fails because its message seems more important to the filmmakers than such petty concerns as plot, character, and cinematic style.
>
> —DAVID ANSEN, *NEWSWEEK*

> Wagner seems determined to have us love her lovers at all costs. No lower-class runaway of the '50s—not James Dean, Sal Mineo, or John Saxon—was ever as excruciatingly "sensitive" as is Travolta. He likes dogs, cries when friends die, refuses to push drugs, and always smiles cutely.
>
> —STUART BYRON, *VILLAGE VOICE*

> Travolta's talent seems more limited than ever . . . convincing evidence that grease is a better lubricant than treacle.
>
> —PHILIP FRENCH, *OBSERVER*, LONDON

> . . . Sounds as if it had originally been conceived for Holly Woodlawn and [*sic*] Joe D'Allessandro . . . so

dumb you keep hoping it is a put-on.

—HOWARD KISSEL, *WOMEN'S WEAR DAILY*

. . . An awful movie, but it may some day occupy a hallowed place in the pantheon of high camp. This isn't your everyday Hollywood boo-boo; the film is downright perverse . . . next to this film, *Grease* looks like *Citizen Kane*.

—FRANK RICH, *TIME*

. . . A movie so embarrassingly awful that it would insult the intelligence of a flea.

—KATHLEEN CARROLL, NEW YORK *DAILY NEWS*

One of the film's few apologists was Rex Reed, then Kathleen Carroll's *Daily News* colleague. He had seen the film before its release, at a screening "so private and so premature that the print wasn't yet dry." He wrote:

Critics who didn't get turkey over the holidays served up generous portions of creamed John Travolta and fricasseed Lily Tomlin. . . . For one thing, the critics aren't

In *Moment by Moment*, Travolta's Strip looks pained and confused, while Tomlin's Trisha is comforting—and dominating.

ready for John Travolta to grow up. They want him zoot-suited and reet-pleated up to his eyeballs in duck grease, white shoes, and disco dumbness, gyrating his pelvis and gushing teenage gibberish. They aren't ready [for him] to cry or tremble or show vulnerability or fall in love, like other mortals. . . . There's more than flim-flam to the Travolta phenomenon, and this film shows his versatility.

The point that eluded Reed was that *audiences*—not critics—were turned off to Travolta in roles like Strip. Feminist issues aside, they did not want the woman on top of Travolta. Even if *Moment by Moment* had been artistically successfully, it would not have suited Travolta's fans. The actor completely miscalculated when he declared, before the film's premiere, "I'm hoping that men can go, 'If it's okay for that character and John Travolta to feel that, maybe it's okay for *me* to feel and

UNIVERSAL PICTURES PRESENTS A ROBERT STIGWOOD PRODUCTION
LILY TOMLIN · JOHN TRAVOLTA "MOMENT BY MOMENT"
EXECUTIVE PRODUCER KEVIN McCORMICK PRODUCED BY ROBERT STIGWOOD
ASSOCIATE PRODUCERS BOB LeMOND AND LOIS ZETTER
WRITTEN & DIRECTED BY JANE WAGNER TECHNICOLOR®
ORIGINAL SOUNDTRACK ON RSO RECORDS AND TAPES

Starts December 22nd at theatres everywhere!

express that.'" A more apt evaluation came from *New York* magazine critic David Denby, who noted, "But if the sensitive man isn't a man any more, if he's emptied of energy, anger, ambition, and sex appeal, it's not much of a victory of sensitivity, is it?"

Until *Moment by Moment*, Travolta only had known success in his career. But now, after being knighted by the press as a major new star in the wake of *Saturday Night Fever*, those same pundits were declaring him a virtual has-been.

He was not the first major star to earn negative reviews. Tony Manero icon Al Pacino, for one, was trashed for his overacting in *Scarface*, and his less-than-memorable presence in *Bobby Deerfield* and *Revolution*. But Pacino was established as a serious stage actor, and his performances in *Serpico*, *Dog Day Afternoon*, and the first two *Godfather* films had firmly rooted his screen career. Films like *Bobby Deerfield*, *Revolution*, and *Scarface* were seen as aberrations, and so he endured professionally.

This was not the case with Travolta. Despite his glowing notices for *Saturday Night Fever*, he still was considered young and relatively untested, all image and little-if-any substance. He may have been compared to Brando, Dean, and Pacino, but the fact was that he was no Brando, Dean, or Pacino. So, after the premiere of *Moment by Moment*, Travolta was the recipient of what he described in 1987 as "the worst press attack that I had ever experienced. Whatever else I encountered later was mild in comparison." It was a pounding which would go way

The dominance/masculinity of Lily Tomlin's character in *Moment by Moment* was stressed in the film's advertising campaign—even to the extent that she is clothed, and he is not. Travolta's fans were not amused.

Travolta and Tomlin in *Moment by Moment*: even his hair is prettier than hers.

beyond the *Moment by Moment* reviews.

Perhaps the press doubted Travolta because he was so good-looking, and had made it big with seeming effortlessness. Some of the career-bashing appeared to be generated by media vultures savoring the opportunity to pick at the carcass of an idol deemed to have fallen on the basis of one miscalculated movie role.

Travolta also was pummeled for distancing himself from the media after being deeply wounded by the critical lambasting of *Moment by Moment*. He may have been pictured up front in the June 1980 issue of *After Dark* magazine, but the Travolta-related cover headline was an ominous one: TRAVOLTA IN TROUBLE? Mike Greco authored the piece inside, headlined: TRAVOLTA TO PRESS: BUG OFF! PRESS TO TRAVOLTA: JOHNNIE, WE HARDLEY KNEW YE. Greco described *Urban Cowboy*, Travolta's *Moment by Moment* follow-up, which was set to open that month, as the star's "comeback film," and he referred to Travolta as an "insecure actor." The writer opined that ". . . he is so afraid of failure that he created an atmosphere on the set reminiscent of the Nixon White House. Travolta surrounded himself with a loyal palace guard who protected him from the enemies and hostile press he fantasized."

The *Urban Cowboy* set was indeed downright unfriendly. Extras were warned that they faced immediate firing if they in any way approached Travolta.

The actor explained his behavior prior to the film's opening: "Let's say I 'went away' emotionally while it was all happening. *Moment* was over and out before I realized *Grease* and *Fever* had happened. I hadn't even enjoyed the first two! *Moment* definitely left me anxiety-prone and frightened. I'm more experienced now. I know how to deal with it all a little better." On another occasion, he declared, "I go through the gamut of emotions a lot: I trust very easily and mistrust very easily. I'm clear, confused, analytical, and add another one—cautious."

Finally, some of Travolta's bad press resulted from alleged avarice on the part of his handlers. An item, published in the March 5, 1979, *New York Post*, began, "Oh, the time demands on a great big star. Take John Travolta, who was asked to cooperate with author Susan Munchour *[sic]* on *The John Travolta Scrapbook*. Sure, said John's managers. Just give us high percentages, control, profits, etc., etc. What was Munchour to get? A one-hour interview with Johnny, with a timer set before them. At the end of the hour, the timer was to go off, at which point, Travolta's managers advised the author, Travolta would get up and leave the room. Munchour declined—and her book, recently published, is doing at least as well as Travolta's ailing career."

Travolta was to go on to enjoy other successes. *Look Who's Talking* became one of the top-grossing films of its year. *Urban Cowboy* and *Blow Out* had their supporters; just as *Pulp Fiction* was reviving Travolta's career, Quentin Tarantino set up a screening of *Blow Out* in Stockholm, to be projected onto an eighty-foot screen—the way he felt the film needed to be seen to be appreciated.

Still, Travolta did not reclaim the level of popularity he had enjoyed at the height of *Saturday Night Fever* and *Grease* for another fifteen years—until 1994, and his reemergence in *Pulp Fiction*.

Clinging to the A-List

Urban Cowboy 1980

Paramount Pictures. Director: James Bridges. Producers: Robert Evans and Irving Azoff. Screenplay: Bridges and Aaron Latham, based on Latham's article in *Esquire* magazine. Cinematographer: Reynaldo Villalobos. Music: Ralph Burns. Editor: David Rawlins. Choreography: Patsy Swayze. CAST: John Travolta *(Bud)*, Debra Winger *(Sissy)*, Scott Glenn *(Wes)*, Madolyn Smith *(Pam)*, Barry Corbin *(Uncle Bob)*, Brooke Alderson *(Aunt Corene)*, Cooper Huckabee *(Marshall)*, James Gammon *(Steve Strange)*, Jerry Hall, Cyndy Hall *(Bar Girls)*, Ann Travolta *(Wedding Party)*, Mickey Gilley, Johnny Lee, Bonnie Raitt, and the Charlie Daniels Band *(Themselves)*. 135 minutes. Rated: PG.

After the debacle of *Moment by Moment*, Travolta made a mini-comeback in *Urban Cowboy*, a film which attempted to re-create the success of *Saturday Night Fever* and place him in the role of cultural trendsetter. Travolta stars as Bud Davis, a character who is to Texas, Gilley's, cowboy hats, mechanical bull-riding competitions, and Johnny Lee's "Lookin' for Love" what Tony Manero is to Brooklyn, 2001 Odyssey, polyester, disco-dancing contests, and the Bee Gees' "Stayin' Alive."

At the outset, farm boy Bud arrives in Houston, where he has come to live with his Uncle Bob and Aunt Corene and find work in a nearby oil refinery. On his first night in town, his relatives introduce him to Gilley's, the real-life "biggest honky tonk in the world," a three-and-a-half acre, shit-kicker cowboy/cowgirl bar. It is here where much of the story takes place. And it is here where he meets pretty cowgirl Sissy (Debra Winger). Bud and Sissy first chat awkwardly, then sashay across the Gilley's dance floor. They kiss. They hug. There is passion between them. And before you can sing a chorus of "Deep in the Heart of Texas," they are married.

The rest of the film charts Bud and Sissy's marital problems, the nadir of which comes when they separate and he takes up with wealthy Pam (Madolyn Smith), a sultry beauty whose "daddy does oil."

Meanwhile, Sissy seeks solace in the arms of Wes Hightower (Scott Glenn), a rough, tough ex-con. Inevitably, Pam—a classic, disposable "other woman" role if there ever was one—bows out when she sees that Bud still loves Sissy. Bud and his fists expose Wes—a classic, disposable villain if there ever was one—as a thief who would rip off Gilley's after losing a mechanical bull-riding competition to Bud. At the finale, Bud and Sissy, presumably, will live happily ever after.

Setting aside the predictability of the plot, the primary failing of *Urban Cowboy* is that Bud and Sissy never become sympathetic charac-

Travolta as Bud, with bottle of Lone Star (rather than the brew that bears his name) in hand, cruising the scene at Gilley's in *Urban Cowboy*.

ters. Bud acts the part of macho lunkhead as he orders Sissy about. When she wants to ride the mechanical bull, he tells her, "It's too dangerous. It ain't for girls." At another point, he yells at her, "Just get me a beer." It's the old husband-is-master, wife-is-slave routine. While Pam may not be a suitable romantic partner for Bud, she does not deserve to be used by him. At no point does Bud undergo the kind of catharsis that makes the finale of *Saturday Night Fever* so appealing. It seems as if, in fashioning the character for Travolta, a conscious attempt was made to create the polar opposite of Strip in *Moment by Moment*.

While not a feminist, Sissy initially comes off as a strong-willed young woman who resists Bud's demands. After they break up, she could move back with her parents, share an apartment with a girlfriend, or even find a place of her own. Instead, she inexplicably stays with Wes, who not only bosses but brutalizes her as well. While just as

The wedding day of Bud and Sissy (Debra Winger). They are pictured with Bud's Aunt Corene (Brooke Alderson) and Uncle Bob (Barry Corbin).

immature as Bud, Sissy is no fool—and she certainly is not sexually attracted to Wes. That she would choose to remain with him just to rile Bud simply is not credible.

Bud may be chauvinistic, but Sissy proves herself to be deceitful, and equally stubborn. They become locked in a game of one-upmanship, but given their personalities and actions, it really is a case of one-downsmanship.

Urban Cowboy is meant to be a showcase for Travolta's sexual charisma. It seems no accident that "Bud" just so happens to rhyme with "stud." At the close of his first evening at Gilley's, he ends up in bed with not one but two sweet, gorgeous young misses. The following evening, he hooks up with Sissy. When he and she squabble in public, Pam is there waiting to fall into his arms, and lead him to her bed.

Only in the movies . . .

During the course of the story, Travolta spends plenty of screen time Texas two-stepping his way across the Gilley's dance floor, by himself as well as with Winger and Smith. His moves and appearance are entirely different from *Saturday Night Fever*, and in this regard *Urban Cowboy* means to be at the vanguard of a newly popular style of dance, music, and dress. The film succeeds in doing for the sounds of Mickey

Gilley, Johnny Lee, Bonnie Raitt, and the Charlie Daniels Band (all of whom appear on screen in performance at Gilley's) what *Saturday Night Fever* did for the Bee Gees. Barkeepers across America began equipping their establishments with mechanical bulls. As reported in *Hollywood: Legend and Reality*, "When John Travolta appeared in *Urban Cowboy* wearing city-slicker rodeo regalia, U.S. jeans sales surged to 600 million pairs."

Offscreen, Travolta became Mr. Urban Cowboy. He was garbed in western gear when, prior to the film's opening, he signed his name in the cement outside Mann's Chinese Theater on Hollywood Boulevard. He traveled to Houston for the *Urban Cowboy* premiere, and the following day came clad for an interview with Liz Smith in what the gossip columnist described as "tan ostrich boots, Levi's, a turquoise and silver belt, and the most beautiful western shirt of pale blue with a cream-colored yolk."

At the time of the opening of *Urban Cowboy*, Travolta was fully aware that his career was in trouble. David Ansen had just reviewed the film positively in *Newsweek*, observing that ". . . Travolta proves right off the bat that he can *play* a cowboy—real or otherwise—from the moment he appears [on-screen] . . ." The actor went on to tell Liz Smith that he "felt Dave Ansen's rave in *Newsweek* was very brave, because it isn't popular to like me these days, and he went out on a limb real early."

As a film, *Urban Cowboy* might be described as moderately successful; at its worst, it is downright silly and lacking in credibility. But Travolta's performance is much more than adequate, and he is as believable as a Texan as he previously had been as a Brooklynite.

Nonetheless, what he did not know at the time was that, with the exception of *Look Who's Talking*, *Urban Cowboy* would be his most successful film until *Pulp Fiction*—almost a decade-and-a-half into the future.

Travolta, Brian De Palma and Nancy Allen, reunited from *Carrie*, on the set of *Blow Out*.

Blow Out 1981

Filmways Pictures. Director-Screenplay: Brian De Palma. Producer: George Litto. Cinematographer: Vilmos Szigmond. Music: Pino Donaggio. Editor: Paul Hirsch. CAST: John Travolta *(Jack)*, Nancy Allen *(Sally)*, John Lithgow *(Burke)*, Dennis Franz *(Manny Karp)*, Peter Boyden *(Sam)*, Curt May *(Donahue)*, John Aquino *(Detective Mackey)*, John McMartin *(Lawrence Henry)*, Deborah Everton *(Hooker)*. 108 minutes. Rated: R.

Travolta next reteamed with Brian De Palma, his director in *Carrie*, for *Blow Out*, a low-rent variation of Antonioni's *Blow-Up* mixed with hints of Hitchcock and Kennedy-assassination-conspiracy theory paranoia.

Blow Out begins with a voyeuristic scene of schoolgirls in an intimate, personal setting, one which is similar to the opening locker room shower sequence in *Carrie*. Here, the kids inhabit a sorority house, where one is shown masturbating while another cavorts nude in the shower as she is approached by a knife-wielding slasher. Cut to Travolta's Jack, sitting with a colleague in an editing room, who laughs about the ineptness of the girl's scream. Jack is a likable, easygoing Philadelphia-based motion picture sound-man, whose credits—*Bloodbath*, *Bloodbath II*, *Bad Day at Blood Beach*, and *Bordello of Blood*—are a slasher film addict's delight.

That night, Jack, with recording equipment in hand, enters a park to capture sounds which he will edit into the film. He soon records a "bang," just before a car careens off a road and into a lake. Jack dives into the water and rescues a drowning passenger: Sally (Nancy Allen), a pretty but none-to-bright young woman who might have been one of Tony Manero's neighbors back in Bay Ridge. Sally is a department store

Jack makes a startling discovery.

cosmetics salesperson who, as it eventually is revealed, had been involved in a sex-and-blackmail scheme being perpetrated on the now-dead driver of the car. What Jack does not know, and is soon to learn, is that the deceased is the governor of his state, who happens to have had higher political aspirations. "That stiff on the stretcher," notes a cop at the hospital, "was probably our next president."

Jack is confounded when the police are unwilling to believe his account of the events, and even eye him suspiciously. A political aide to the governor tells him to "forget you ever saw" Sally. "It's better the governor died alone. . . . We don't want to embarrass his family. . . ."

Blow Out means to be an examination of reality-versus-fantasy. Prior to becoming a soundman, Jack had a job in which he wired policemen who were working undercover. After a mishap which resulted in the death of one of his cops, he retreated into the world of celluloid make-believe. Now, reality has intruded on Jack's life once again, in the form of his witnessing this tragedy. What follows is a convoluted mystery, filled with superficial melodramatics and more plot holes than Swiss cheese, in which he relives the "accident" and concludes that the "bang" he heard was a shot, rather than a tire blow out.

Jack finds himself a lone seeker of truth as he attempts to uncover the facts and unravel the mystery of the politician's death. The authorities, rather than examining the evidence, inexplicably regard him as a wacko, a conspiracy theorist. The connection between this tragedy and the Kennedy assassination is at first hinted at, and then becomes all-too obvious when it is observed that the various pieces of evidence in the case comprise "the biggest thing since the Zapruder film."

Travolta is quite believable as Jack, and without a doubt *Blow*

Out features his most mature performance to date. In 1985, Margy Rochlin, in a preface to her talk with Travolta in *Interview* magazine, observed, "As uneven a film as *Blow Out* was, Travolta inhabited his role with an eerie credibility, drawing upon none of the macho swagger that had served him so well in the past."

But the film bombed at the box office. Decent performances in disappointing movies are quickly forgotten—and so was Travolta's work in *Blow Out*.

Staying Alive 1983

Paramount Pictures. Director: Sylvester Stallone. Producers: Stallone and Robert Stigwood. Screenplay: Stallone and Norman Wexler, based on characters created by Nik Cohn. Cinematographer: Nick McLean. Music: The Bee Gees, Frank Stallone, and Johnny Mandel. Editors: Don Zimmerman and Mark Warner. Choreography: Dennon Rawles and Sayhber Rawles. CAST: John Travolta *(Tony Manero)*, Cynthia Rhodes *(Jackie)*, Finola Hughes *(Laura)*, Steve Inwood *(Jesse)*, Julie Bovasso *(Mrs. Manero)*, Frank Stallone *(Carl)*. 96 minutes. Rated: PG.

In order to jump-start his career, Travolta backtracked to familiar territory for his next project, *Staying Alive*, a sequel to *Saturday Night Fever*. While his performance as Tony Manero cannot be faulted, the film failed to alter his fading fortunes. What Travolta needed was a new character to play who was as striking as Tony, not a retracing of familiar territory.

Staying Alive begins where *Saturday Night Fever* leaves off to the extent that Tony has abandoned the Brooklyn of his youth. Four years have passed since the finale of *Fever*, in which Tony and Stephanie solidified their friendship. But the character of Stephanie is missing from *Staying Alive*. "I think [Tony] probably got tired of Stephanie after about six months," Travolta noted at the time of the film's release.

Tony may have been a star at 2001 Odyssey, but in Manhattan he is one of a horde of struggling young stage gypsies who regularly auditions unsuccessfully for dancing roles. "It's like you're invisible," he notes, of the audition process. "They don't even see you." Tony subsists in a fleabag hotel on West 46th Street, and waits tables and teaches a dance class.

When it comes to his specialty, Tony has maintained his confidence and self-esteem. "Be proud. You're dancers. You love dancing," he tells his class. The women still are hot for him, as nameless sexy young females tell him how they love to watch him walk and invite him up to their apartments in the wee hours of the morning. But Tony is not interested. He only has Broadway on his mind—and the two women who play key roles in the scenario.

The first is Jackie (Cynthia Rhodes), whom Tony has known for some time, a Broadway gypsy who "has been in and out of choruses for six years." Jackie is sweet and pretty, and devoted to Tony, but she is unexceptional; she lacks the talent ever to get beyond the chorus line.

Enter Laura (Finola Hughes), the film's "Stephanie" character. Laura is not only beautiful but also a well-connected, multitalented featured dancer who rides around town in chauffeured limousines. She speaks with a British accent, which Tony immediately misconstrues as intelligence and class.

Tony is entranced by Laura and begins pursuing her and ignoring Jackie: a plot device which mirrors his behavior toward Stephanie and Angie, the marriage-obsessed girl from *Saturday Night Fever*. The difference between Stephanie and Laura is that the *Saturday Night Fever* heroine was appealingly vulnerable beneath her shell, while Laura is never more than a one-dimensional bitch. And Jackie is in no way manipulative like Angie. When she sees that Tony's priorities lie elsewhere, she breaks off with him. Jackie has more of a sense of self than Angie. She does not scheme to trap Tony into what inevitably would be a loveless relationship.

At one point, Tony observes that, since moving to Manhattan, he has a "new mature outlook on life." But the fact is that he still is Tony Manero, semi-articulate Brooklyn Italian-American stud who has conveniently forgotten any lesson he learned at the end of *Saturday Night Fever* regarding how to treat women. As the scenario plays itself out, he must relearn this as he comes to appreciate Jackie's appeal.

Professionally speaking, Tony wins a job in the chorus of a new musical titled *Satan's Alley*, described by its director as "a journey through hell that ends with an ascent to heaven." Laura is the show's featured dancer, while Jackie is in the chorus. But success as a gypsy is insufficient for Tony. Conveniently, Laura's dance partner proves too "mechanical" for the part. Tony practices his routine, and asks to be his replacement. The director "has a feeling" about "the kid," so Tony gets the role and, at the finale, a star is born on Broadway. *Staying Alive* ends with a reprise of the Bee Gees "Stayin' Alive," with Tony strutting down Broadway in the same manner as he did at the beginning of *Saturday Night Fever*. These sequences serve to bookend both films. Once upon a time, Tony Manero owned the streets of Bay Ridge. Now, after much struggle, he owns the streets of Broadway.

If the dramatic aspects of *Staying Alive* are uninspired and predictable, the film is done in by its finale. *Satan's Alley* is a mindbogglingly gauche, overproduced show, crammed with laughable theatrics and enough artificial smoke to close down an airport. It resembles an extended, tacky Las Vegas production number, something more in line with a routine from *Showgirls* than a legitimate Broadway musical. Of course, its opening night audience applauds wildly, as if they are wit-

nessing the premiere of *Oklahoma!*
or *The King and I* or *A Chorus Line*.

Travolta cannot be faulted
for any of the film's failings. He
dances far more in *Staying Alive*
than in *Saturday Night Fever*, and
much of what he does on the dance
floor is spectacular. From every
voice inflection and body movement, he knows and thoroughly
understands the character of Tony
Manero. One cannot imagine any
other actor playing the role.

In the overall scheme of
Travolta's career, however, *Staying
Alive* has to be considered just as
disappointing as the Bee Gees'
songs on the soundtrack, which—except for the "Stayin' Alive"
reprise—are collectively bland and forgettable. While still able to earn
star-status, Travolta no longer was the hot young actor whose every on-
screen appearance was considered an event.

Travolta's Tony Manero strikes a
balletic pose during the *Satan's
Alley* finale.

Finally, in *Staying Alive*, Sylvester Stallone, the film's director
(and Travolta's longtime friend), pulls an Alfred Hitchcock. Near the
film's beginning, he is seen on-camera, briefly brushing shoulders with
Tony Manero on a crowded midtown Manhattan street.

Two years after the release of *Staying Alive*, Travolta was asked if
he would consider filming *Saturday Night Fever III*. "Maybe," he
responded. "It depends upon how interesting it could be. . . . But I guess
if I were to do a sequel, Tony could be a choreographer. Maybe he could
go to Hollywood and do movies."

But *Staying Alive* was to be the cinematic swan song of Tony
Manero.

Fourteen

The Travolta Physique

While preparing to play Tony Manero in *Saturday Night Fever*, Travolta at first honed his dance floor moves with a member of the disco group Dancing Machine. Eventually, he took dancing lessons for three hours each day, and worked out for an additional two with Sylvester Stallone's personal trainer, an ex-boxer who had guided the actor through his star-making turn in *Rocky*. "When I started," Travolta told Rex Reed, "I couldn't even do one of the knee bends I do in the film." By the time the cameras rolled, Travolta had lost over twenty pounds. Prior to playing Tony Manero, he even patronized Brooklyn discos—including 2001 Odyssey, where he would observe the on and off-the-dance-floor behavior of the young Italian Stallions—and entered several dance competitions.

This regimen was but a prelude to the one he undertook while readying for *Staying Alive*. "You see," he explained during the film's production, "back in the last week of July 1982, I was in the play *Mass Appeal*, with that marvelous Charles Durning, in Snowmass, a little town near Aspen, Colorado. There was a nice gym facility there, and I knew that Ballet West was in Aspen at the time. I was out of shape and overweight, and this was the perfect setup for me. I worked out every day at the gym, had ballet lessons three times a week with Sharee Lane at Ballet West, and did the show in the evening. I had a long way to go."

Eventually, under Stallone's guidance, Travolta embarked on a half-year-long program of dancing and weight lifting. He pumped iron for two-and-a-half hours a day, and danced for three more. His diet consisted of fish, chicken, or turkey with a green salad and fresh fruit, and was supplemented by multivitamins. He drank Perrier, juice, and Emergen-C, a vitamin drink. He waxed the hair off his arms, darkened his skin with a tanning machine—and emerged with a muscled, finely sculpted physique. His weight was reported to be 161 pounds.

Prior to the release of *Staying Alive*, Travolta explained his reason for keeping fit by declaring, "I think it's maintenance with me. In other words, it's part of my job to have a particular appearance . . . I mean, I think if you see a gut, you'd probably not find that much interest in my physical appearance in all honesty, and the mirror would be [a] very little part of my life."

In 1984, Travolta authored an exercise book, titled *Staying Fit!* and published by Simon and Schuster. It was described as "his complete program for reshaping your body through weight resistance training and modern dance techniques." "It's pretty much what I did to train for *Staying Alive*," he told columnist Liz Smith. "I got so much fan mail after I changed my body that I thought I ought to put it down for others." Smith reported that while Travolta no longer exercised daily, he still worked out four times a week.

Minus body hair and in peak physical condition, Travolta replays Tony Manero in *Staying Alive*.

Following Travolta's subsequent career decline, he no longer preserved his physique. "I'm fairly big on eating—and I don't like exercise," he admitted in 1989. By that time, the thirty-five-year-old actor's weight had risen to 190 pounds, and he came complete with love handles. The following year, he ballooned to 224 pounds—most of which he had lost by the time he began filming *Pulp Fiction*.

As Travolta was approaching forty, his body had become that of an average middle-aged man. At one point in *Pulp Fiction* he bares his chest. He is neither fat nor flabby; the best word to describe his physical state is fleshy. The Travolta bod on view in *Staying Alive* was as much a part of the past as the popularity of leisure suits. Indeed, writer Fred

Travolta's Tony Manero, in *Saturday Night Fever,* is garbed only in black bikini underwear.

Schruers began a February 1996 *Rolling Stone* profile, published as Travolta turned forty-two, with the line, "Call him anything but late for dinner." Today, the actor employs a full-time chef, and admittedly relishes dining on the tastiest foods, finest wines, and sweetest deserts.

"In some ways, I like how I look now, because it gives more texture to [my] characters," he declared in 1995. "I like how I've aged. And I like a little more weight on me. I have a lot of young qualities, so I think the weight and the age kind of cuts it nicely—on-screen, that is . . ."

Fifteen

More Career Woes

Two of a Kind 1984

Twentieth Century-Fox. Director-Screenplay: John Herzfeld. Producers: Roger M. Rothstein and Joe Wizan. Cinematographer: Fred Koenekamp. Music: Patrick Williams. Editor: Jack Hofstra. CAST: John Travolta *(Zack)*, Olivia Newton-John *(Debbie)*, Charles Durning *(Charlie)*, Beatrice Straight *(Ruth)*, Scatman Crothers *(Earl)*, Castulo Guerra *(Gonzales)*, Oliver Reed *(Beazley)*, Richard Bright *(Stuart)*, Vincent Bufano *(Oscar)*, Toni Kalem *(Teri)*, James Stevens *(Ron)*, Jack Kehoe *(Chotiner)*, Ernie Hudson *(Detective Staggs)*, Warren Robertson *(Himself)*, Deborah Dalton *(Angie)*, Tony Crupi *(Detective Bruno)*, Robert Costanzo *(Captain Cinzari)*, Ann Travolta *(Bank Teller)*, Kathy Bates *(Furniture Man's Wife)*, Gene Hackman *(Voice of God)*. 87 minutes. Rated: PG.

On paper, *Two of a Kind* seemed like a sure-fire hit. It reteamed Travolta with Olivia Newton-John, his costar in *Grease*; not without irony, it was known as *Second Chance* during its production. But this new film and its predecessor were in no way two of a kind. *Grease* may be an entertaining film, but cinematically speaking it is no landmark. However, when contrasted to *Two of a Kind,* it takes on the status of *Gone With the Wind.*

Two of a Kind sinks the moment it opens, as the camera speeds through puffy white clouds. God (depicted via a ray of light, and with the voice of Gene Hackman) has returned from vacation to find the world "a total mess." He has decided to "start over" by flooding the earth. A quartet of angels attempts to convince him not to take such dire action. God agrees, but only if they can prove that two self-centered, unscrupulous earthlings are capable of sacrificing themselves for each other, and falling hopelessly in love.

Travolta appears as the first of this chosen pair: Zack, a slick dude garbed in tight-fitting pants, purple shirt, and cool-looking shades. Zack is an inventor who has not had much success in marketing his gadgets—perhaps because they are as inspired as the edible sunglasses which

Travolta reteamed with Olivia
Newton-John in *Two of a Kind*.

are a part of his fashion statement.

Unable to pay the $13,464 he owes a mobster, he attempts to
steal the money from a bank, but Debbie (Newton-John), an unemployed actress moonlighting as a bank teller, laughs at him as his fake
mustache begins to fall off. She then outfoxes Zack by pilfering the
money, while all he gets to take is the blame.

By this time, you either are laughing at the inanity of the plot or nodding off to sleep with boredom as you glance at the clock on your VCR and wonder how much longer the film will last.

Zack and Debbie do just as the angels have promised, in spite of the interference of Beazley (Oliver Reed), a dapper devil. The scenario hits one of its many nadirs when Zack transforms the act of screwing in the doorknob of Debbie's apartment into a metaphor for raw sex.

Two of a Kind is excruciating to watch. The best that can be said for it is that Travolta and Newton-John are attractive. At one point, as he attempts to seduce Newton-John, Travolta removes his shirt to reveal the bare chest and toned body that is a holdover from *Staying Alive*. Soon afterward, as Zack and Debbie spend a romantic day afloat on a ferry in New York Harbor, there are a couple of shots of the Brooklyn Bridge—as if the bridge's presence somehow will conjure up the magic of *Saturday Night Fever*. But a bare chest, a toned body, and the Brooklyn Bridge do not necessarily make a good movie.

Zack, in his comical bank robbery disguise.

Perfect 1985

Columbia Pictures. Director-Producer: James Bridges. Screenplay: Bridges and Aaron Latham, based on articles by Latham in *Rolling Stone*. Cinematographer: Gordon Willis. Music: Ralph Burns. Editor: Jeff Gourson. CAST: John Travolta *(Adam Lawrence)*, Jamie Lee Curtis *(Jessie Wilson)*, Jann Wenner *(Mark Roth)*, Anne De Salvo *(Frankie)*, Laraine Newman *(Linda)*, Marilu Henner *(Sally)*, Matthew Reed *(Roger)*, Carly Simon *(Herself)*, Tom Schiller *(Carly Simon's Friend)*, Ann Travolta *(Mary)*, Sam Travolta *(Hotel Desk Clerk)*, David Paymer *(Managing Editor)*, Lauren Hutton *(Herself)*. 120 minutes. Rated: R.

Ace *Rolling Stone* reporter Adam
(Travolta) confers with his editor
(Jann Wenner) and photographer
(Anne De Salvo) in *Perfect*.

erfect is anything but. The best that can be said for it is that it is
not the total disaster of *Two of a Kind*. Combined, however,
both films added significantly to the damage already done to
Travolta's career by *Moment by Moment*.

After *Perfect*, there would be no more second chances
for the actor, no *Urban Cowboys* or *Blow Outs*. *Perfect*, which
reunited Travolta with *Urban Cowboy* director James Bridges,
was to be his final major Hollywood release in the first phase
of his career.

Travolta's role is that of a character he might have known in real
life: Adam Lawrence, a pushy, hard-nosed reporter for *Rolling Stone*
magazine. (In the late 1970s, a real-life *Rolling Stone* journalist reportedly
shattered the window of Travolta's car after not being allowed additional interview time.) Adam is meant to be a brilliant and dedicated professional; he even leaves his computer on all night, just in case he conjures
up a few nocturnal inspirational thoughts for his readers. His stories
consistently are marked by controversy. He has recently published one
on Carly Simon, whom he happens to meet in a restaurant. "I read that
shit you wrote about me," she tells him, just before tossing a bloody
mary in his face.

At present, Adam is closing in on an exclusive interview with a
computer magnate who recently was arrested on drug charges, and who

Travolta and Jamie Lee Curtis, starring in a less-than-perfect *Perfect*.

is claiming the State Department framed him because he was negotiating to sell his product to an Iron Curtain country. At the same time, Adam decides to investigate a story with a trendier angle: how health clubs are becoming the singles bars of the 1980s. He begins his research at a Los Angeles club called the Sports Connection, where he is attracted to sexy Jessie Wilson (Jamie Lee Curtis), an ex-Olympic swimmer who is described as "the aerobics pied piper" and "probably the best female instructor" at the club. Adam is genuinely interested in Jessie, but his journalistic instincts take over as he attempts to interview her for his exposé. As Jessie is a less-than-willing subject, he decides instead to focus on Linda (Laraine Newman), one of the Sports Connection's regulars, a lonely and vulnerable woman who is characterized as the club's most "used piece of equipment." At the finale, Adam manages to maintain his journalistic integrity while realizing that the exploitation of other peoples' lives to sell magazines is neither morally nor ethically defensible. By doing so, he wins Jessie, and the two—as Bud and Sissy in *Urban Cowboy* and Zack and Debbie in *Two of a Kind*—live happily ever after.

    Perfect means to be hip, with-it, cutting-edge, as it strives to examine the lifestyle and professional and personal conflicts of an investigative reporter and the impact of his writing on the lives of his subjects. However, for the most part, *Perfect* wallows in pretension and superficiality. This is never more so as Adam spouts to Jessie his ideas about baby boomers and "Emersonian America," and breathlessly ends his spiel by telling her, "You are so hot." Coming in second in the silliness sweepstakes is the observation that "Mikie Douglas is in town," made by Adam's editor, Mark Roth (played by real-life *Rolling Stone* editor Jann Wenner). Throughout the film, Adam and his colleagues have endlessly affected, rushed telephone conversations, with the phone becoming a weapon (rather than a means) of communication.

Perfect, additionally, is a voyeur's delight. At one point early on, Adam takes one of Jessie's aerobics classes. The purpose of this extended sequence is to show off Travolta's body and cue audiences in on how sexy and in-shape he is as he duplicates Curtis's pelvic motions. During the sequence, Travolta appears to have an erection underneath his shorts. The result is worse than pornography. It is a tease.

In 1996, just as his film, *Broken Arrow*, was set to go into release, Travolta was interviewed in *Rolling Stone* and *Playboy* magazines. Not unexpectedly, the *Rolling Stone* piece cites only *Staying Alive* and *Two of a Kind* as Travolta's 1980s career-wreckers. Regarding *Perfect*, the magazine conveniently quotes Travolta as declaring that the film "did work on various levels. I think it's a film to be reevaluated." Meanwhile, the interviewer in *Playboy*, a *Rolling Stone* competitor, refers to *Perfect* as "a messy flop that struck a blow to [Travolta's] career." Regarding the film, the actor explains, "Everyone held high expectations for that film, because it was from the same director and writer as *Urban Cowboy*. I took it because of the people involved, even though there were problems with the script. I still thought it was going to be pretty good."

In 1985, the year in which *Perfect* was released, Travolta became the 1,805th celebrity to have his name placed on a gold star on the Hollywood Walk of Fame. Yet for the next few years, he chose to put his career on hold. "I was burned out after those films," he declared in 1987, referring to *Perfect*, *Two of a Kind*, and *Staying Alive*. But he claimed that their quality was not the reason. "It wasn't the movies so much as the publicity tours after the movies," he said. "I must have done fourteen hundred interviews. If you had told me two years ago that I would never have to work again, I would have said 'Great.'"

Sixteen

A Return to His Roots

The Dumb Waiter 1987

ABC. Director-Producer: Robert Altman. Screenplay: Harold Pinter,
based on his play. Cinematographer: Pierre Mignot. Music: Judith
Gruber-Stitzer. Editor: Helene Girard. CAST: John Travolta *(Ben)*, Tom
Conti *(Gus)*. 48 minutes.

After the disaster of *Perfect*, and two years away from his last
acting job, Travolta chose to return to the medium in which
he first won fame. Gary Pudney, vice president and senior
executive in charge of specials for ABC, had known Travolta
since his *Welcome Back, Kotter* days. He suggested the actor to
Robert Altman, who was mounting for the network a drama-
tization of *The Dumb Waiter*, Harold Pinter's one-act play,
which originally had been produced in London in 1960.
Altman initially was dubious about the choice, but was charmed by
Travolta as the pair "did lunch" and was happy to offer him the job.

He and Tom Conti play Ben and Gus, a pair of oddball hit men
who arrive at a dilapidated old mansion. Ben is a Cockney who sports a
garish vest and tie and looks like an extra from *Guys and Dolls*. Gus is
especially seedy, with greasy, slicked-down hair. The two men bicker
and jabber back and forth, mostly about inconsequentials. Apparently
they are hiding out. They have just pulled some kind of a job—at one
point, Ben reads a tabloid headlined AUSSIES BLASTED BY DEADLY
DUO—and are awaiting instructions for their next assignment.

Suddenly a sealed envelope is mysteriously tossed into their
room. Then a creaky old dumbwaiter drops from above. On it is a note
requesting "two teas without sugar." Other, similar messages follow, all
delivered via the dumbwaiter. One is for "soup of the day, liver, and
onions." Another is for a macaroni dish, and still another is for scampi.
It is as if Ben and Gus are cooks in a restaurant, only they aren't—and,
anyway, they are lacking the elements necessary to fulfill the orders.

At one point, Ben imagines shooting himself with a gun. Soon

97

Travolta and Tom Conti in *The Dumb Waiter.*

afterward, Gus leaves the room to get a glass of water. Upon his return, he is shot by Ben.

The Dumb Waiter is a cryptic piece, to say the least. The characters of Ben and Gus are only rudimentally drawn, and the source of the meal requests is never revealed. The play, ultimately, is an allegory about the master-servant relationship—a popular Pinter topic—and an examination of the manner in which people relate to one another, and use the English language.

Prior to its airing, *The Dumb Waiter* was screened at the Museum of Broadcasting in New York. Present were Travolta, Conti, Altman, and Pinter. "I found Mr. Pinter's words so effortless and easy to do as an actor," Travolta declared during a seminar following the screening, adding, "I just know that I had a *ball* doing [the piece]. It was maybe my favorite thing I've ever done." Earlier, he had contrasted *The Dumb Waiter* to his film projects when he told the *New York Times*, "The pressure was off, that's everything in a nutshell. It was like being Off-Broadway again. No high stakes, no twenty million dollars breathing down your neck. You're doing it for the sake of doing it."

Travolta makes a believable Cockney thug, and his performance might have revved up his career. Alas, *The Dumb Waiter* was a made-for-TV drama and, back in the 1980s, with-it movie actors simply did not accept roles on television shows. Travolta's casting, no matter how prestigious the project, was considered a come-down. The fact was that, back in 1987, in order to secure a decent role, Travolta had to return to television: a medium which he had abandoned for a decade.

Seventeen

Direct-to-Video Hell

The Experts 1987

Paramount Pictures. Director: Dave Thomas. Producer: James Keach.
Screenplay: Nick Thiel, Steven Greene, and Eric Alter, based on a story
by Greene and Alter. Cinematographer: Ronnie Taylor. Music: Marvin
Hamlisch. Editor: Bud Molin. CAST: John Travolta *(Travis)*, Arye Gross
(Wendell), Kelly Preston *(Bonnie)*, Deborah Foreman *(Jill)*, James Keach
(Yuri), Charles Martin Smith *(Bob Smith)*, Jan Rubes *(Illyich)*, Brian
Doyle Murray *(Jones)*, Mimi Maynard *(Mrs. Smith)*, Eve Brent *(Aunt
Thelma)*, Rick Ducommun *(Sparks)*, Steve Levitt *(Gil)*, Tony Edwards
(Nathan). 83 minutes. Rated: PG-13.

Travolta returned to moviemaking with *The Experts*, a charmless, low-rent *Dumb and Dumber*–style comedy. This film is so
incredibly insipid (when not downright dull) that it only briefly
played in theaters in Texas, Colorado, and Oklahoma before
becoming the first of Travolta's direct-to-video throwaways.
What's more, its point-of-view is that of a movie that was politically correct for 1952: it is okay to be stupid, just so long as
you have the freedom to be so in the good old U.S.A.

Travolta and Arye Gross star as Travis and Wendell, two slick-
dressing but otherwise luckless New York City nitwits who are hot to
open their own nightclub. Opportunity comes when they are recruited
by KGB honcho "Bob Smith" (Charles Martin Smith) to relocate to
Indian Springs, Nebraska, where they will manage a New York style
club.

The catch is that Indian Springs actually is located in Russia. It
is "the most secret KGB complex in the world," a replica of an
American small town where Soviet spies-to-be are trained to live like
Americans.

The film's premise is that Indian Springs is trapped in a 1950s
time warp. All of the Russians are learning about an America from the
era of *Grease*. There are no video stores. No joggers. No punk rock. No
sushi bars. No heavy metal. No *Rolling Stone* magazine. Smith has hired

The best that can be said for *The Experts* is that Travolta met his future wife, Kelly Preston, in preproduction. They are pictured with costar Arye Gross.

Travis and Wendell to "modernize" Indian Springs, so that its "residents" will not go into culture shock when they are sent out on assignment.

New York City may be more on the cutting edge of contemporary pop culture than the Andy Hardyville that is Indian Springs, but Travis and Wendell are too dim-witted to realize that a small midwestern town could not be steeped *that* far back in the past. The obvious story line plays itself out as the boys accidentally discover the truth of their situation, and all ends happily as the now liberty-loving, consumerism-adoring Indian Springs "citizens" are airlifted to freedom in America.

The most interesting part of *The Experts* comes at the opening of the boys' club, when Travis attempts to enliven the crowd by clapping his hands, shaking his body, and jumping about to some danceable contemporary music. "Is this a joke?" he asks. "Doesn't anyone here know how to dance?" (He may as well be asking, "Hasn't anyone here ever seen *Saturday Night Fever*?") Enter sexy Bonnie (Kelly Preston), a KGB operative assigned to become Travis's girlfriend. "I know how to dance," she tells him, and they begin performing a highly erotic routine.

This sequence, ever so plainly, is meant to re-create Travolta's *Saturday Night Fever* dance floor sex appeal. While he still may have the right moves, it is no longer 1977. The makers of *The Experts* failed to acknowledge that the Travolta of 1977 and 1978 already had been consigned to the cinema and pop culture history books.

More important, it was while shooting *The Experts* that Travolta first met Preston, whom he later would marry. One might think that fiction and fact become blurred as Preston's Bonnie first seduces Travolta's Travis. As she rips off his pants and shirt, Travolta easily might be breaking character when he looks directly at the camera and declares, "Is this a terrific girl or what!"

Chains of Gold 1989

Academy. Director: Rod Holcomb. Producer: Jonathan D. Krane. Screenplay: John Petz, Linda Favila, Anson Downes, and John Travolta. Cinematographers: Dariusz Wolski and Bruce Surtees. Music: Trevor Jones. Editor: Chris Nelson. CAST: John Travolta *(Scott Barnes)*, Marilu Henner *(Jackie)*, Joey Lawrence *(Tommy Burke)*, Bernie Casey *(Sergeant Falco)*, Ramon Franco *(James)*, Hector Elizondo *(Lieutenant Ortega)*, Benjamin Bratt *(Carlos)*, Conchata Ferrell *(Martha)*, Tammy Lauren *(Rachel)*, Raphael Rey Gomez *(Bobby)*. 95 minutes. Rated. R.

Society, as depicted in *Chains of Gold*, has come a long, sorry way since the times of *Grease* and *Saturday Night Fever*. Way back when, tough kids basically were harmless, or were the perpetrators of acts that hurt no one but themselves. However, the teens in *Chains of Gold*—and there are many of them—have more than just attitude. They are foot soldiers in a gang of vicious, deadly crack dealers. They are like Hitler Youth, with their Führer being Carlos, a smooth, tough, twenty-one-year-old who brags that his evil dealings have made him worth $25 million.

Chains of Gold intends to be a sobering look at the effect of poverty on impressionable young people, and the responsibilities adults must take on in molding the lives of children. Unfortunately the result is little more than a corny, violence-laden, by-the-numbers inner-city actioner.

Travolta plays Scott Barnes, an ex-advertising man and alcoholic whose life slipped downward after the death of his son. In his mind, he was responsible for the boy's demise, because he was "too drunk to pull him out of that car" after a traffic accident.

Now Scott toils as a social worker. He despises his bureaucratic, paper-shuffling boss, and he really wants to have a positive impact on the lives of his clients. One of them is thirteen-year-old Tommy, who has become Scott's substitute son. (Tommy is played by Joey Lawrence, whom Travolta would later cite as being the ideal candidate to play Vinnie Barbarino in a movie version of Welcome Back, Kotter.)

Tommy basically is a good kid, but he has been enticed by the lure of easy money and become a member of Carlos's gang. After trying to extricate himself from his situation, he is kidnapped and imprisoned. In order to save Tommy, Scott tries to infiltrate the gang, and he becomes a Stallone- and Schwarzenegger-like superhero, dodging bullets and errant cars and, most ludicrously, surviving a fall into a pit of hungry alligators.

The role of Scott Barnes is meant to be a departure for Travolta, even to the extent that he shuns dancing. At one time—before his son's death—he may have been a social butterfly. But now, as he motions to a dance floor, Barnes observes, "This, you know—it's not me."

Chains of Gold was supposed to have been released to theaters. But it collected dust on the shelf for a couple of years before debuting on the Showtime cable television network, eventually making its way into video stores.

Eyes of an Angel 1989

Trans World Entertainment.
Director: Robert Harmon.
Producers: Michael Phillips and
Chris Chesser. Screenplay: Robert
Snitzel. Cinematographer: Theo
Van de Sande. Music: Randy
Edelman. Editors: Donn Cambern
and Zach Staenberg. CAST: John
Travolta *(Bobby)*, Ellie Raab *(The
Girl)*, Tito Larriva *(Cissy)*, Jeffrey
DeMunn *(Georgie)*, Richard Edson
(Goon), Vincent Guastaferro
(Goon), Tripoli *(The Dog)*. 91 minutes.
Rated: PG-13.

Travolta and Ellie Raab in *Eyes
of an Angel.*

Eyes of an Angel is yet another career drop. Filmed in 1989 under the title *The Tender*, and co-executive produced by Michael Douglas for Paramount Pictures, it remained unreleased—and deservedly so—until after Travolta's comeback in *Pulp Fiction*. Its story is dumb. It is not entertaining on any level. It would be useful, however, as a teaching tool in cinema classes, to be cited as an example of how not to go about writing and directing a movie.

Travolta plays Bobby, a down-and-out ex-con and widower who, like Scott Barnes in *Chains of Gold*, has conquered a drinking problem. Bobby lives in a cold-water flat in Chicago—by the train tracks, no less—with his waiflike young daughter (Ellie Raab, billed in the credits as "The Girl"). Bobby's brother-in-law is a slimy, conniving thug who stages illegal dog fights. "The Girl" befriends one of the dogs, a Doberman, who survives being dumped into the river after losing a fight. When Bobby and "The Girl" are forced to take it on the lam to Los Angeles, the super-pooch—incredibly—follows them cross-country, eventually becoming the savior of "The Girl" and Bobby.

Eyes of an Angel is meant to be inspiring, but instead it is muddled and hokey—and as believable as a three-dollar bill.

Boris and Natasha: The Movie 1990

MCEG Productions. Director: Charles Martin Smith. Producer: Jonathan D. Krane. Screenplay: Charles Fradin, Linda Favila, and Anson Downes, based on a story by Fradin and Brad Hall and on characters created by Jay Ward for *The Bullwinkle Show*. Cinematographer: Daryn Okada. Music: David Kitay. Editors: Patrick Kennedy and Maysie Hoy. CAST: Sally Kellerman *(Natasha Fatale)*, Dave Thomas *(Boris Badanov)*, Andrea Martin *(Toots)*, John Calvin *(Harve)*, Paxton Whitehead *(Anton/Kregor Paulovitch)*, Larry Cedar *(Mr. X/Willie)*, Christopher Neame *(Fearless Leader)*, Alex Rocco *(Sheldon Kaufman)*, Anthony Newley *(Sal Manelli)*, John Travolta *(John Travolta)*, John Candy *(Kalishak)*, Charles Martin Smith *(Hotel Clerk)*. 88 minutes. Rated: PG.

Travolta makes a cameo appearance in this tepid live-action comedy about Boris Badanov (Dave Thomas) and Natasha Fatale (Sally Kellerman), the inept Cold War–era spies from Pottsylvania who were first seen as animated characters a quarter-century earlier menacing Rocky and Bullwinkle on television. Like *Chains of Gold*, it was meant to be released to theaters, but debuted instead on Showtime.

The scenario involves Boris and Natasha's coming to America to seek out a "time-reversing microchip." Thirty-seven minutes into the film, Travolta appears out of nowhere, ringing the door of their hotel suite and presenting himself as a suitor to Natasha.

While not billed in the opening credits, Travolta is listed in the closing ones as having played "John Travolta."

If you sneeze, you will miss him.

Shout 1991

Universal. Director: Jeffrey Hornaday. Producer: Robert Simonds. Screenplay: Joe Gayton, from his story. Cinematographer: Robert Brinkmann. Music: Randy Edelman. Editor: Seth Flaum. CAST: John Travolta *(Jack Cabe)*, James Walters *(Jesse Tucker)*, Heather Graham *(Sara Benedict)*, Richard Jordan *(Eugene Benedict)*, Linda Fiorentino *(Molly)*, Scott Coffey *(Bradley)*, Glenn Quinn *(Alan)*, Frank von Zerneck *(Toby)*, Michael Bacall *(Big Boy)*, Sam Hennings *(Travis Parker)*, Charles Taylor *(Deputy)*, Gwyneth Paltrow *(Rebecca)*, Kristina Simonds *(Rachel)*. 89 minutes. Rated: PG-13.

Jack Cabe (Travolta) is an inspiration to Jesse Tucker (James Walters) in *Shout*.

hout—called *Midnight Rider* while in production—is not a very good movie. It is illogical, with a thoroughly implausible story line. But it is fascinating for the manner in which Travolta is depicted on screen. If Tony Manero was on the cutting edge of disco, and Danny Zuko was a nostalgic 1950s greaser, Jack Cabe—his character in this film—is meant to epitomize the birth of rock 'n' roll.

It is set in the rural Texas of the early 1950s. Its focus is on Jesse Tucker (James Walters), a rebellious teen who has established a reputation for being "a handful" in his brief tenure at a combination school/work camp for orphaned or troublesome adolescent boys. Jesse and his comrades are bossed about by the overseer, Mr. Benedict (Richard Jordan), a character out of a 1930s chain-gang movie. During the course of the story, Jesse becomes romantically and sexually involved with Benedict's beautiful daughter Sarah (Heather Graham).

Cabe appears from out of nowhere and takes a job as the boy's new music teacher. He plays a mean blues harmonica and promptly

Despite the focus of the *Shout* scenario on Jesse's evolving relationship with Sara (Heather Graham), Travolta's character did have a love interest. She is played by Linda Fiorentino (pictured with Travolta), who had not yet heated up the screen in *The Last Seduction*.

educates his charges in a new kind of music, which is rooted in the funky backwoods dance halls whose customers are almost exclusively black. That music has a name: rock 'n' roll. Cabe tells the boys that it is here to stay, as it soon will "burn through this country like a prairie fire." Cabe is a mythical figure who, it eventually is revealed, is wanted for murder. But that crime was justified, as he killed "a white man while defending a colored man in Biloxi, Mississippi."

The character of Jesse and the manner in which he grows through the story is meant to mirror Tony Manero in *Saturday Night Fever*. Jesse is cocky and spirited. At first, girls are no more than sex objects; he willingly bets his pals that he will "nail" Sara Benedict, the film's substitute "Stephanie." But romantic feelings grow within him. Jesse comes to realize that Sara is more than just a sexual receptacle, and that he can have a more mature and fulfilling relationship with her.

Meanwhile, Cabe, who becomes Jesse's mentor, is supposed to invoke memories of Manero and Danny Zuko as he dances ever-so-briefly with his adult romantic counterpart (Linda Fiorentino).

Shout is meant to be an homage to Travolta. But all it did was mire him in the past. What he needed, yet again, was a re-formation of his image, a revitalization of his screen personality.

And that is where Quentin Tarantino steps in.

Eighteen

Look Who's in a Hit Film

Look Who's Talking 1989

Tri-Star Pictures. Director-Screenplay: Amy Heckerling. Producer:
Jonathan D. Krane. Cinematographer: Thomas Del Ruth. Music: David
Kitay. Editor: Debra Chiate. CAST: John Travolta *(James)*; Kirstie Alley
(Mollie), Olympia Dukakis *(Rosie)*, George Segal *(Albert)*, Abe Vigoda
(Grandpa), Bruce Willis *(Voice of Mikey)*, Twink Caplan *(Rona)*, Joan
Rivers *(unbilled; Voice of Julie)*.
93 minutes. Rated: PG-13.

Look Who's Talking Too 1990

Tri-Star Pictures. Director: Amy Heckerling. Producers: Jonathan D.
Krane and Bob Gray. Screenplay: Heckerling and Neal Israel.
Cinematographer: Thomas Del Ruth. Music: David Kitay. Editor:
Debra Chiate. CAST: John Travolta *(James Ubriacco)*, Kirstie Alley *(Mollie
Ubriacco)*, Olympia Dukakis *(Rosie)*, Elias Koteas *(Stuart)*, Twink Caplan
(Rona), Bruce Willis *(Voice of Mikey)*, Roseanne Barr *(Voice of Julie)*,
Damon Wayans *(Voice of Eddie)*, Mel Brooks *(Voice of Mr. Toilet*
Man), Gilbert Gottfried *(Joey)*, Lorne Sussman *(Mikey)*, Paul Shaffer
(Taxi Businessman).
81 minutes. Rated: PG-13.

Look Who's Talking Now 1993

Tri-Star Pictures. Director: Tom Ropelewski. Producer: Jonathan D.
Krane. Screenplay: Ropelewski and Leslie Dixon, from the characters
created by Amy Heckerling. Cinematographer: Oliver Stapleton. Music:
William Ross. Editors: Michael A. Stevenson and Harry Hitner. CAST:
John Travolta *(James Ubriacco)*, Kirstie Alley *(Mollie Ubriacco)*, David
Gallagher *(Mikey Ubriacco)*, Tabitha Lupien *(Julie Ubriacco)*, Lysette
Anthony *(Samantha)*, Olympia Dukakis *(Rosie)*, Danny DeVito *(Voice of
Rocks)*, Diane Keaton *(Voice of Daphne)*, George Segal *(Albert)*, Charles
Barkley *(Himself)*, John Stocker *(Sol)*, Elizabeth Leslie *(Ruth)*.
97 minutes. Rated: PG-13.

Not all of Travolta's pre–*Pulp Fiction* films were of the quality of *Shout*, *Eyes of an Angel*, or *Chains of Gold*. *Look Who's Talking* is an amiable romantic comedy whose surprise box-office success resulted in two sequels. Still, Travolta was considered a fallen star, a perception which remained unchanged despite his participation in these films. The first *Look Who's Talking*, like *Shout*, is designed as an ode to Travolta past. Because it is such, it did nothing for his career in the present.

Kirstie Alley stars as Mollie, a thirtysomething Manhattan accountant who has been sleeping with Albert (George Segal), a married client. For an eternity, Albert has been promising to leave his wife for Mollie. And for an eternity, he has been procrastinating. Then one day, Mollie discovers she is pregnant. Albert is excited by the prospect of impending fatherhood, and leads Mollie to believe that she can expect his support. But Albert is an inveterate womanizer. During the latter stages of her pregnancy, he informs her that he is in love with someone else. "I'm going through a selfish phase right now," is his lame excuse.

Travolta plays James, the cab driver who happens to transport Mollie to the hospital when she goes into labor. When he asks her if she is doing her "Lamaze breathing," you know he is a concerned, unselfish adult who would be a suitable romantic partner for Mollie and co-parent for her child. (During its production, the film was, for good reason, known as *Daddy's Home*.) James is taken with Mollie and Mikey, her baby boy. He becomes Mikey's babysitter, and sets out to convince

Mollie that he would make an excellent stepfather. Because James is a lowly cab driver, Mollie is reluctant to view him as husband material. She fantasizes their life together as being mired in poverty, with James aging into a belching blue-collar stereotype. But Mollie comes to realize that, despite his career status, James would make "the best daddy there is" for Mikey. Like thousands of other celluloid couples, Mollie and James "meet cute." Then they squabble, squabble, squabble—before falling in love and getting married.

Look Who's Talking is a gimmick film, with the thoughts and quips of Mikey, from prebirth to birth to toddlerhood, cleverly communicated to the audience via the unmistakable voice of Bruce Willis. Of course, none of the adult characters hear what he is saying; only the viewer does, resulting in much of the film's good humor. The baby-voice device is played right through to the finale, as Mikey is presented with a little sister, Julie, courtesy of Mollie and James—and her voice is that of Joan Rivers, who blurts out her tagline of "Let's talk."

In *Look Who's Talking*, Travolta gives a charming performance. His James is at once a likable nice guy and a sweeter, more mature version of the characters that made him famous. He is ultracool as he handles Mikey, and as he attempts to romance Mollie. And of course, he gets to dance: a sexy mini-routine with Mollie, done to Gene Pitney's "Town Without Pity" (rather than a number from *Saturday Night Fever* or *Grease*).

Finally, James just so happens to live in Englewood, New Jersey, Travolta's hometown. Had Travolta not become "John Travolta, Movie Star," he might have aged into a real-life James, a husband/father/working-stiff cab driver who never leaves Englewood.

Despite several positive test screenings, Tri-Star had such little faith in *Look Who's Talking* that it almost did not release the film theatrically. Yet it went on to become one of the year's top moneymakers, earning $55 million and placing eighth on *Variety*'s list of Big Rental Films of 1989. "There's only one movie that I got to see before anyone

Saturday Morning Fever: in *Look Who's Talking*, James bonds with Mikey.

else judged it and that I deemed funny and successful and definitely a hit," Travolta recalled in 1995, "and that was *Look Who's Talking*."

However, the talking-baby gimmick begins to evoke yawns in *Look Who's Talking Too*, a charmless, unfunny sequel rushed into production upon the success of its predecessor. The birth of Julie is replayed, but here her voice is that of Roseanne (billed as Roseanne Barr). Joining her and Willis are the voices of Damon Wayans as Eddie, Mikey's toddler pal, and Mel Brooks, as a talking toilet bowl. This time around, the baby and toddler chatter is flat and crude, with much of the humor based on the children uttering words like "asshole" and "schmuck." The almost plotless film has the James who was so endearing in *Look Who's Talking* becoming far less likable. He and Mollie now are mostly thoughtless and obnoxious. At its worst, *Look Who's Talking Too* is one long, shamelessly manipulative commercial for various toys, toy stores, foods, beverages, and clothing. The film's sole entertaining moments come when Travolta leads Mikey and other toddlers in a routine inspired by Elvis Presley's famous dance number from *Jailhouse Rock*.

The second sequel, *Look Who's Talking Now*, is an improvement over its predecessor, but remains well below the level of the original. Mikey and Julie have become young children who can speak on their own, so a pair of dogs, voiced by Danny DeVito and Diane Keaton,

have the majority of the comic lines. Travolta dances again: he does a box step and a South American routine with Lysette Anthony (an Olivia Newton-John lookalike who plays his vampish new boss), and he and Kirstie Alley appear in a Fred-and-Ginger-inspired number, dancing to the tune of "The Very Thought of You."

Look Who's Talking Now desperately tries to exploit the comic formula established in Look Who's Talking, with its makers hoping that audiences will be satisfied by the mere presence and natural appeal of cute children and animals.

Homage to Elvis: In *Look Who's Talking Too*, Travolta , joining with Mikey and other pre-schoolers, recreates a bit of the choreography in Elvis Presley's most famous celluloid dance number, from *Jailhouse Rock*.

Otherwise, those who have paid their money to sit through the film might realize that the rest of the material is paper-thin, and only intermittently funny.

Despite the box-office numbers of the Look Who's Talking films, Travolta's career became stalled to the point where he stopped receiving movie offers. The films were, after all, not Travolta vehicles. Audiences flocked to them not to see him, but to be entertained by talking infants and dogs. In fact, in Look Who's Talking he does not even appear on screen for the first half-hour.

Travolta was considered a star of the past, if not a flash-in-the-pan. His role in Look Who's Talking, after all, might have been played by any number of actors. His bankability was zero, and for the first time he was seriously concerned for the future of his career. "I thought, 'Oh, man, is it over?'" he reported—just as Pulp Fiction was set to make its bow in New York.

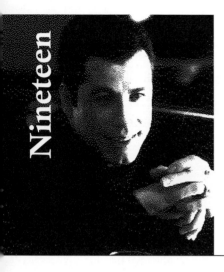

Nineteen

A Star is Reborn

Pulp Fiction 1994

Miramax Films. Director-Screenplay: Quentin Tarantino. Based on sto-
ries by Tarantino and Roger Avary. Producer: Lawrence Bender.
Cinematographer: Andrzej Sekula. Editor: Sally Menke. CAST: John
Travolta *(Vincent Vega)*, Samuel L. Jackson *(Jules Winnfield)*, Uma
Thurman *(Mia)*, Harvey Keitel *(The Wolf)*, Tim Roth *(Pumpkin)*,
Amanda Plummer *(Honey Bunny)*, Maria de Medeiros *(Fabienne)*, Ving
Rhames *(Marcellus Wallace)*, Eric Stoltz *(Lance)*, Rosanna Arquette *(Jody)*,
Christopher Walken *(Koons)*, Bruce Willis *(Butch)*, Quentin Tarantino
(Jimmie). 154 minutes. Rated: R.

In *Pulp Fiction* and his subsequent feature, *Get Shorty*, Travolta ages
into a super-hip contemporary Bogart-Cagney-Robinson-Garfield.
His characters, Vincent Vega and Chili Palmer, are tough, stylishly
suave, and cool-under-fire. As in *Saturday Night Fever* and *Grease*,
they exude a self-assured machismo. But the key difference is that
they are far more worldly (not to mention more corrupt) than
Barbarino-Manero-Zuko. As Vega and Palmer, Travolta radiates a
quiet self-confidence. He is fun to watch as he commands the
screen, offering full-blown, movie-star turns. In *Pulp Fiction* in particular,
Travolta all at once reinvents his screen persona and resuscitates his
career.

Pulp Fiction is stylish and irreverently hip, one of the most
praised and popular movies of 1994. It is named for the sensationalistic
crime novels and dime-store magazines whose heyday came between
the 1920s and 1950s. While regarded as pop culture throwaways at the
time of their publication, they were spawning a new type of American
literature: lurid, noirish depictions of crime and sin in the shadowy city,
often featuring cynical, determined detective heroes. The most famous
practitioners of pulp fiction—among them Dashiell Hammett,
Raymond Chandler, and Jim Thompson—became legendary writers, as
important to the history of American arts and letters as Hemingway,
Fitzgerald, or Faulkner.

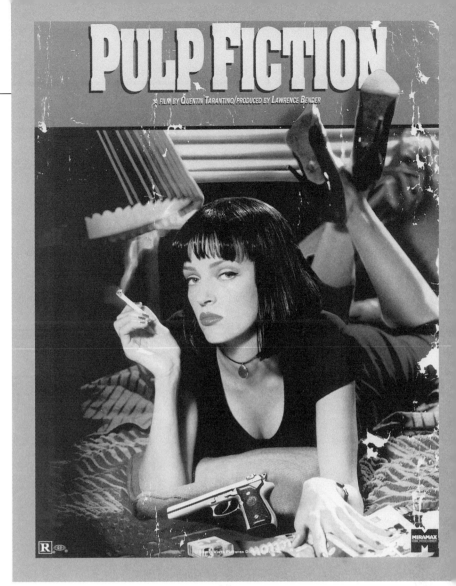

As *The Piano* and *The Crying Game* in previous years, *Pulp Fiction* was the happy beneficiary of a media frenzy. When one entered the press office at the 1994 Toronto Film Festival, the subject of the first conversation loud enough to over-hear was "Quentin"—as in director-screenwriter Tarantino—and *Pulp Fiction* was not even on the festival's programming slate. Upon strolling through the aisles of Tower Video on Manhattan's Upper West Side just before the film's release, two young cinéastes were overheard loudly discussing the merits of Tarantino's previous feature, the instant cult classic *Reservoir Dogs*, and the hype surrounding *Pulp Fiction*. To fully understand the fascination with Tarantino among younger, hipper movie audiences, all one had to do was roam the film-related Internet bulletin boards. One would find note after note on Tarantino: detailed analysis of the *Reservoir Dogs* characters and their motivations; expectations regarding *Pulp Fiction*; opinions as to why Tarantino was the most audacious and original American filmmaker since Martin Scorsese made his splash with *Mean Streets* two decades earlier.

Travolta's participation in *Pulp Fiction* is as a part of an ensemble. His Vincent Vega is a beefy, sociopathic hit man and heroin addict who comes complete with shoulder-length hair and an earring in his right earlobe. The scenario interweaves three stories concerning various thugs, lowlifes, and desperate characters, including Vega; Jules Winnfield (Samuel L. Jackson), his Bible-spouting sidekick; Marcellus Wallace (Ving Rhames), their crime-lord boss; Mia (Uma Thurman), Marcellus's wife; Lance (Eric Stoltz), a drug dealer, and Jody (Rosanna

Vincent Vega, in a classic Tarantinoesque pose. © Miramax Buena Vista.

Arquette), his wife; Butch (Bruce Willis), an on-the-lam boxer, and Fabienne (Maria de Madeiros), his lover; and Koons (Christopher Walken), a Vietnam veteran. Lastly, there is the film's most charismatic character: The Wolf (Harvey Keitel), a no-nonsense "problem-solver" who can remove all evidence from the grisliest crime scene quicker than you can watch an episode of *NYPD Blue*. The film is book-ended by a robbery in a diner perpetrated by a pair of young and amoral lovers (Tim Roth, Amanda Plummer), who call each other Pumpkin and Honey Bunny. They might as well be the same duo Tarantino conjured up for Oliver Stone's *Natural Born Killers*.

All of these characters are not so much human beings as creations culled from earlier, vintage gangster films and film noir dramas. Vega might have been one of the wiseguys played not by a De Niro or Pacino but by a Garfield, Bogart, Cagney, or George Raft—with the addition of R-rated dialogue, blood-soaked killings, and the fact that Vega has a yen for primo heroin. He might be Bogie or Cagney reincarnated as he stares at Butch and quietly barks at him. "You ain't my friend, palooka. . . . I think you heard me fine, punchy." He is a meat-and-potatoes hood who responds unsympathetically when Jules soulfully talks of giving up "the life" to wander the earth and experience adventures. To his mind, Jules will have become nothing more than a bum. Vega is unimpressed when Mia takes him to Jack Rabbit Slim's, an outrageous upscale 1950s-style combination nightclub-eatery that is steeped in nostalgia for the era's pop culture heroes. "I think it's like a wax museum with a pulse," he declares.

Travolta and Uma Thurman tango in *Pulp Fiction*. © Miramax Buena Vista.

While in the company of Mia, Vega is charming. In their scenes together Travolta and Thurman play off each other beautifully; they are a reincarnation of Bogie and Bacall. Upon reviving her after she overdoses on heroin, they agree that Marcellus need never know what has happened. As they part company, he elegantly blows her a kiss.

But primarily, Vega is stubborn and belligerent—even when he messes up royally. After accidentally blowing the head off a passenger in a car, Vega is quick to place the blame on Jules, the driver, by telling him, "You went over a *bump* or something." As The Wolf rattles off orders to him and Jules, setting in motion a plan that will result in their self-preservation, Vega insists that their savior say "please."

Through the course of their on-screen time, Vega and Jules share in memorable repartée, some of which is calm and some not-so-calm. They debate the difference between giving a woman (or, as they would say, a "bitch") a foot massage and performing oral sex on her, and what

Jules calls "miracles" and Vega dubs "freak occurrences." They discuss the merits of pigs versus dogs, and the variations in the manner in which McDonald's serves its meals in Europe and America.

Their fast-food conversation was instant classic movie dialogue. Vega has just returned to Los Angeles after spending three years in Europe, on assignment in Amsterdam. He and Jules chat while driving to complete a murderous assignment for Marcellus Wallace:

Vega: And you know what they call a Quarter Pounder with Cheese in Paris?

Jules: They don't call it a Quarter Pounder with Cheese?

Vega: No, man, they got the metric system. They wouldn't know what the fuck a Quarter Pounder is.

Jules: Well, what do they call it?

Vega: They call it a *Royale* with Cheese.

Jules: *Royale* with Cheese?

Vega: That's right.

Jules: What do they call a Big Mac?

Vega: A Big Mac's a Big Mac, but they call it *le* Big Mac.

Jules: *Le* Big Mac! What do they call a Whopper?

Vega: I don't know. I didn't go to Burger King.

While each story focuses on specific individuals, characters from the other episodes suddenly appear to play key roles. Vega and Jules are featured in a preface to Part One, garbed in black suits, blacks ties, and white shirts, as they go about the business of disposing of some young men who are behind in drug money payments to Marcellus. The crux of Part One, titled "Vincent Vega & Marcellus Wallace's Wife," is the

evening Vega spends with Mia. He has been ordered by Marcellus, who is out of town, to be her escort. This assignment is riskier than his usual tough guy-enforcer jobs, because any hint of impropriety between him and the vampish Mia will result in his instant demise.

The *Pulp Fiction* script, as the one for *Grease*, is loaded with pop cultural references. This is never more the case as Vega and Mia dine at Jack Rabbit Slim's, which might have been a set for a scene in *Grease*. However, neither Frankie Avalon, Eve Arden, nor Edd Byrnes appear. Instead, an Ed Sullivan impersonator is the maitre d', and announces the club's entertainment. A clone of Ricky—not Rick—Nelson strums a guitar and sings. Marilyn Monroe, Buddy Holly, and Mamie Van Doren imitators wait tables. Movie posters of *Motorcycle Gang* and *Attack of the 50-Foot Woman* decorate the walls.

Vega's and Mia's table is the interior of a vintage car. He orders a "Douglas Sirk steak, bloody as hell." She selects a "Durward Kirby burger, bloody," and a "five-dollar shake." Their waiter, "Buddy Holly," asks if she wants it "Martin and Lewis" (vanilla) or "Amos and Andy" (chocolate). She selects the "Martin and Lewis."

The Jack Rabbit Slim's sequence is just one of the film's many odes to pop culture. Butch the boxer might be the grandson of John Garfield in *Body and Soul*, Kirk Douglas in *Champion*, or Robert Ryan in *The Set-Up*. Koons the Vietnam vet is an ex-POW who seems to be in a

Jules Winnfield (Samuel L. Jackson), Vincent Vega (Travolta) and The Wolf (Harvey Keitel), in *Pulp Fiction.* © Miramax Buena Vista.

time warp from *The Deer Hunter* (which just so happened to have featured Christopher Walken). He offers a monologue in which he refers to a GI named Winocki, which is the name of the character played by Garfield in the 1943 war film *Air Force*. In two sequences featuring Vega using bathrooms, the book he reads is *Modesty Blaise*, based on Peter O'Donnell's popular British comic strip about a female secret agent.

At Jack Rabbit Slim's, Vega and Mia share some striking dance floor moves. "Ed Sullivan" announces the start of the "world famous Jack Rabbit Slim's twist contest." "Wanna dance?" Mia asks. From the look on Vega's face, you would think that she has made an indecent proposal. "No, no, no, no. . . ." he responds, in what may be taken as yet another ironic cinematic reference to Travolta's dancing proclivity in *Saturday Night Fever*. But Mia insists. "Now I wanna dance. I wanna win. I wanna win that trophy. So dance good."

Before walking onto the dance floor, Vega removes his shoes. Will this be another classic Travolta dance moment? Will it become 1977 all over again as the Bee Gees take over the soundtrack and Travolta finds himself instantaneously garbed in a white suit? Not at all. The music is Chuck Berry; Jack Rabbit Slim's, after all, is designed as an ode to the pop culture of the 1950s and early 1960s, not the late 1970s.

Vega and Mia perform a slick, cool twist, with Vega/Travolta forming **V**'s with his fingers and running them across his eyes: a gesture first seen ever-so-briefly on *Welcome Back, Kotter*. These moves are reminiscent of Travolta's dancing bits in *Look Who's Talking*, *Shout*, and *The Experts* in that they are reminders of his dancing skills. The difference is that we are watching a new, vastly more mature Travolta, not a character who is a shell of his old screen persona.

(This sequence was parodied in *Spy Hard*, a 1996 descendant of *Airplane!* featuring Leslie Nielsen as intrepid secret agent Dick Steele and Nicolette Sheridan as fellow agent Veronique Urkinsky. After first meeting, they comically converse over a table in the "Fantasee" night-

Travolta twists the night away in *Pulp Fiction*. He had first used the "V" gesture as Vinnie Barbarino, performing in a talent competition on *Welcome Back, Kotter*. © Miramax Buena Vista.

club. In a flash, they are aping Travolta's and Thurman's dance floor moves. Both are dressed like the characters they are lampooning, with Nielsen's get-up topped off by a white wig with ponytail. The sequence ends all too soon, however, upon the arrival of some villains.)

Upon their return to her house, contest trophy in hand, Mia and Vega do a mini-Valentinoesque tango through the door. Vega tells himself that all he will do is have a drink and leave. But intimacy between the two becomes immaterial when Mia, who has been snorting cocaine all night, overdoses on heroin, and Vega goes into overdrive as he saves her life—and his skin.

(Buena Vista/Miramax Home Video released *Pulp Fiction* to video in September 1995. Six months later, the title was remarketed with the addition of two outtakes, introduced by Tarantino. One features Butch the boxer. The other is of a sequence in which Mia videotapes Vega at the outset of their "date." She yaps on and on, asking him if he is related to Suzanne Vega, if he favors Elvis or the Beatles, if he prefers Peter Strauss or Nick Nolte in *Rich Man, Poor Man*. . . . Her final question: If he were Archie, who would he rather fuck, Betty or Veronica? In his responses, Vega initially is uncomfortable and subdued, to the point where he seems to be nodding out. But he does not resist Mia's queries, and becomes more intrigued as they add up.)

Vega and Jules are among the key participants in Part Three, "The Bonnie Situation," as an accidental killing bloodies up the back seat of their car and necessitates their contacting The Wolf. Vega appears in the middle section, titled "The Gold Watch," a minidrama involving Butch. But here, he is little more than a bit player. He is seen briefly in Butch's apartment, where he has been dispatched by Marcellus to rub out the boxer. Butch, who has returned there to retrieve his father's watch, catches Vega off guard. The hood's weapon is in the kitchen, and Butch hears him flushing the toilet. Vega exits the bathroom and—*boom*—he instantly becomes a corpse, with his blood splattered across the bathroom door. His billing in the credits of this sequence might be little more than "mobster in bathroom."

Despite the brevity of his appearance in "The Gold Watch," and the fact that he is surrounded by equally impressive actors in the other sequences, Travolta and his performance were the talk of the 1994 Cannes Film Festival. This was where *Pulp Fiction* premiered, and walked off with the Palme d'Or. Travolta saw the film for the first time in Cannes, at a screening with two thousand others in attendance. During a series of round-robin press interviews the day following the showing, he was not so much queried as lionized. After years of neglect from the press, here he was back at center stage. He later admitted that he was so overcome by emotion that he felt like crying—which is exactly what he did.

A star had been reborn. Several months later, by the time *Pulp Fiction* had been announced as the opening night selection at the New York Film Festival, Travolta had solidly reclaimed his spot as a major Hollywood player.

Twenty

Tarantino on Travolta (and *Pulp Fiction*)

I n person, Quentin Tarantino is refreshingly unpretentious, as animated and talkative as any of his weirded-out characters. He answers questions in a stream-of-consciousness monologue. His sentences are fractured, not so much because he is unable to speak correctly as because he is brimming with ideas and enthusiasm. Jay Leno, while interviewing Uma Thurman on *The Tonight Show*, was not exaggerating when he described Tarantino as "sort of a manic guy."

"Some of the [*Pulp Fiction*] characters were written for specific actors," Tarantino explained at the 1994 New York Film Festival. "Pumpkin and Honey Bunny were written for Tim Roth and Amanda Plummer. The Wolf was written for Harvey Keitel. In other cases, I wanted to find the right person for the part.

"I didn't write it for John," he continued, referring to Vincent Vega. In fact, Tarantino originally was considering for the role Michael Madsen, who had acted for him in *Reservoir Dogs*. "I met [Travolta] two-thirds of the way through the writing [of the script]. I'd been told that he was a big fan. When I was a kid, it seemed like he was the top movie star in the world. In the course of having lunch together, it was like, wow, he'd be a good Vincent Vega. This also was the case with Mia. I was in love with this character, but I didn't know what she looked like. I tried black actresses, white actresses, older ones, younger ones. None were right. I had dinner with Uma and, boom, I knew I'd met her."

The Travolta-Tarantino luncheon took place in January 1993 at the restaurant in the Four Seasons Hotel in Beverly Hills. Travolta agreed to meet with Tarantino after some amount of prodding from his agent, and because he was taken by the filmmaker's zeal. The purpose of their meeting was not to discuss job possibilities.

Tarantino, as one will not be surprised to learn, is an avid collector of movie and TV-related memorabilia. After the lunch, he invited Travolta to his apartment in a week's time. In what was the irony of ironies—an inventive press agent could not have conjured up a more clever yarn—Tarantino's apartment proved to be the very same one Travolta had rented back in 1974, when he first came to Los Angeles.

The pair hung out, and they played the board games based on Travolta's 1970s hits. The actor offered to compete in the characters of Zuko/Manero/Barbarino, but Tarantino preferred him to play as himself. To Tarantino's way of thinking, Travolta was no dusty relic of the past. Zuko/Manero may exist on video store shelves, and Barbarino soon would be revived via Nick-at-Nite reruns, but Travolta was very much alive, and very much an entirely separate entity.

Afterward, Tarantino returned to writing *Pulp Fiction*. As he honed the character of Vega, he kept thinking of Travolta. Eventually he began reworking the role to accommodate Travolta, who six months later received the completed script while in Vancouver shooting *Look Who's Talking Now*.

Tarantino was determined to cast the fallen idol, insisting that he only would make the film with Travolta as Vincent Vega—even though he could have selected other, more bankable actors for the role. At the New York Film Festival, Travolta only noted the obvious when he declared that he "wasn't exactly the 'actor of the year.' Quentin was having trouble convincing people that I could do it. He fought for me." While Travolta had been thinking that his career might be over, he never for once doubted his talent. Of his work in *Pulp Fiction*, Tarantino added, "One of the things that was very cool was that I didn't even realize how good his performance was until I began editing. I then called him up, and told him, 'Wow, you *really* are good in this.'"

Tarantino's other casting choices mirrored motion picture history. "Regarding Butch, Bruce [Willis] really brings to mind 1950s actors, people like Aldo Ray, Ralph Meeker. The young Robert Mitchum. The young Kirk Douglas. That's just the look I wanted for Bruce."

While he proudly declared that he can "break down every movie by genre or subgenre," Tarantino noted that his films are to a certain degree reality-based. "I guess what I do is similar to the way many

Travolta and Quentin Tarantino.
© Miramax Buena Vista

actors act," he said. "I may create a character out of little bits of some-one I might know or see. Sure they come from what I've seen [on-screen] or read, but it's also about my friends, my relatives. My main concern is my characters. I'm always asked, 'How far will I go with vio-lence?' I can only say that I don't know. I don't want to put any limita-tions on my characters. My only obligation is to be true to them."

While insisting that he has incorporated his personal experi-ences into his scripts, Tarantino will not write about them in a literal sense. "Let's say I break up with a girl, and I'm all messed up over it," he explained. "That may find its way into a piece, even if that piece is about soldiers taking over a chateau during World War Two." Similarly, the primary force behind *Pulp Fiction* is not pulp fiction writing. "The influence actually is J. D. Salinger," he said. "From his writing, I got the idea of doing the three different stories and how the characters move in and out of them. After all, any of these stories could have been a movie unto itself."

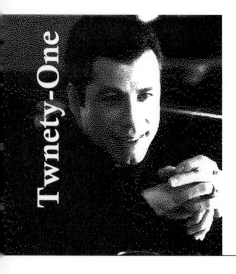

Twenty-One

Not a Flash-in-the-Pan

Get Shorty (1995)

Metro-Goldwyn-Mayer. Director: Barry Sonnenfeld. Producers: Danny DeVito, Michael Shamberg, and Stacey Sher. Screenplay: Scott Frank, based on the novel by Elmore Leonard. Cinematographer: Don Peterman. Music: John Lurie. Editor: Jim Miller. CAST: John Travolta *(Chili Palmer)*, Gene Hackman *(Harry Zimm)*, René Russo *(Karen Flores)*, Danny DeVito *(Martin Weir)*, Dennis Farina *(Ray "Bones" Barboni)*, Delroy Lindo *(Bo Catlett)*, James Gandolfini *(Bear)*, Jon Gries *(Ronnie Wingate)*, Renée Props *(Nicki)*, David Paymer *(Leo Devoe)*, Martin Ferrero *(Tommy Carlo)*, Miguel Sandoval *(Mr. Escobar)*, Jacob Vargas *(Yayo Portillo)*, Linda Hart *(Fay Devoe)*, Bobby Slayton *(Dick Allen)*, Ron Karabatsos *(Momo)*, Barry Sonnenfeld *(Doorman)*, Bette Midler *(Doris)*, Harvey Keitel and Penny Marshall *(Themselves)*. 105 minutes. Rated: R.

With *Get Shorty*, based on the Elmore Leonard best-seller, Travolta could not have made a wiser choice for a *Pulp Fiction* follow-up. (Ironically, he first turned it down, and had to be convinced to accept it—by Quentin Tarantino, along with Danny DeVito, his costar and the film's coproducer.) Just as Vinnie Barbarino, Tony Manero, and Danny Zuko are variations of the same character, Travolta's Chili Palmer is a mutation of Vincent Vega. Palmer is a cool, hip gangster (albeit not a druggie, and far brighter than Vega); he starts out as a Miami-based loan shark who puts the muscle on chumps who have not met their markers. Palmer may be a criminal but, as Vega, he is meant to be a likable one. "I think you're a decent type of man," a character observes of him early on, "even if you are a crook."

What adds to the fun of *Get Shorty* is that Palmer is an inveterate movie buff. At one point, he decks Bear (James Gandolfini), a ruffian and former stuntman, in a parking lot. When the lug regains consciousness, Palmer asks if he is okay. When he nods in the affirmative, Palmer inquires, "So how many movies have you been in?" The answer:

approximately sixty. "What are some of them?" Palmer continues.

    Get Shorty, as *Pulp Fiction*, is loaded with pop cultural references. A *Thin Man* poster hangs on a wall in Palmer's Miami office. He is constantly dropping the names of, and reciting dialogue from, classic movies, from *Touch of Evil* to *Cabin in the Cotton* to *Rio Bravo*.

    The premise of *Get Shorty* is a clever one. If, as we all know, Hollywood is a community made up of frauds, sharks, and con artists, then a real-life criminal should be able to reinvent himself and succeed behind the camera—let alone use his life experience to coach an actor playing a gangster.

    The plot involves Palmer's finding himself in Los Angeles, where his knack for persuasion proves to be ideally suited to a career as a movieland mover and shaker. His initial contact is Harry Zimm (Gene Hackman), a schlock film producer whose credits include the likes of *Grotesque*, *Slime Creatures*, and *I Married a Ghoul From Outer Space*—films in which Travolta's character in *Blow Out* might have worked as the soundman. Palmer has come west to collect a gambling debt from Zimm, who is attempting to finance his next project. Zimm may live in

Rene Russo, Travolta, Gene Hackman and Danny DeVito (bottom, clockwise from left), the super-hip stars of *Get Shorty*.

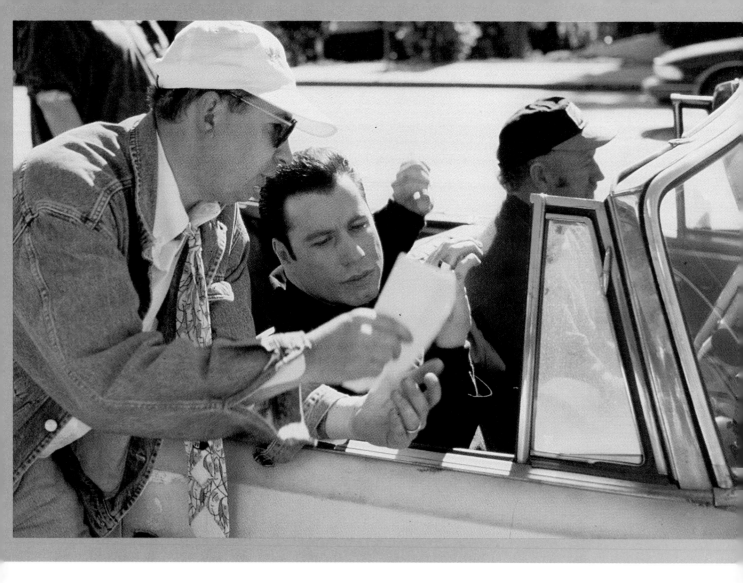

Gene Hackman, Travolta, *Get Shorty* director Barry Sonnenfeld (right to left).

a world of tinseltown fantasy, but his monetary problems are very real. At the same time, he shares Palmer's love of old movies. He senses that a union with the gangster—no papier-mâché tough guy, but the real thing—will allow him to solve his financial dilemma and secure the services of Martin Weir, super-hot actor (Danny DeVito, the "shorty" of the title, a character supposedly modeled after Dustin Hoffman). Palmer is enticed by the idea of making it in Hollywood, and the two link up as coproducers of Zimm's project. The mobster-turned-mogul promptly befriends and beds Zimm's leading lady (René Russo), and in one of the film's highlights, offers Weir an amusing lecture on how to act tough and put forth attitude.

Two other hoods are forces in the scenario. The first is Miami-based Ray "Bones" Barboni (Dennis Farina). He is determined to recover a $300,000 insurance payoff that has been stashed in an airport locker, a situation which serves as a running gag throughout the film. The other, Bo Catlett (Delroy Lindo), is from Southern California. Zimm also is indebted to him, and he, too, is eager to make movies. After all, he notes, "What's the point of living in L.A. unless you're in the movie business?"

Get Shorty, as *Pulp Fiction*, features an outrageously hip, off-the-wall sense of humor. This extends to references to the Travolta of old, one example of which is the phrase "dead as disco." Unlike similar touches in the actor's pre–*Pulp Fiction* films, they do not seem to be pressing for a sense of false nostalgia—primarily because *Get Shorty* is, on its own, a richly entertaining film. Additionally the film works as a clever Hollywood satire. Its script is filled with knowing barbs which you do not have to be a Hollywood insider to understand. Everybody knows that the screenwriter is the least-appreciated member of a film's creative team: At one point, it is noted that the only way a writer ever can earn serious money is by authoring a ransom note. Later on, Weir meets Palmer and several others for lunch. In minute detail, the actor describes to a waiter the manner in which he wants his eggs cooked—yolkless, as he is health-conscious. He generously orders portions for the entire table, yet is long gone before the arrival of the less-than-appetizing meal.

In *Get Shorty*, Travolta essentially repeats his *Pulp Fiction* performance. However, here, his character does not experience a similar, gruesome fate. Chili Palmer ends up not just a player but a powerbroker in the movie business, one with his own private space in a major studio parking lot, right next to that of Penny Marshall.

Most important of all for Travolta, his success in *Get Shorty*—which was number one at the box office in its first week of release, pulling in just over $12.6 million—proved to any naysayer that his *Pulp Fiction* triumph was no aberration. As *Washington Post* critic Desson Howe so aptly observed in his review of the film, "This comic potboiler about gangsters in Hollywood would be a great piece of fun even without Travolta. But as a loan shark from Miami with a charming bedside manner and big-time movie dreams, he raises the fun quotient into the sublime."

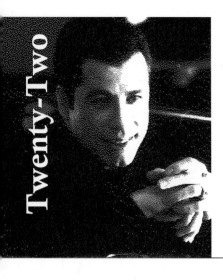

Twenty-Two

Travolta and Cagney

Chili Palmer, Travolta's *Get Shorty* character, would be the ideal proprietor of a movie revival house. If he were to open such a theater, he could screen movies starring one of Hollywood's most beloved tough guys, and Travolta's most admired actor: James Cagney.

In 1942, Cagney surprised audiences who only knew him for his dramatic roles with a spirited, Oscar-winning performance as turn-of-the-twentieth-century vaudeville and musical comedy star George M. Cohan in *Yankee Doodle Dandy*—a clip of which also is featured in *That's Dancing!* Travolta has stated that *Yankee Doodle Dandy* is his favorite movie; among his other top films are *The Godfather*, *Cabaret*, *That's Entertainment*, and the French-language romantic drama *A Man and a Woman*, which back in 1966 was everybody's favorite date movie.

The careers of Cagney and Travolta are similar in that both started out as stage hoofers, and both were equally adept at dancing across the screen and playing tough guys. As far back as 1980, their stardom and appeal were compared by *Newsweek*, which noted that Travolta was to his era "what Cagney was to the Depression: the common man [or man-child] with that extra savvy that sets him apart."

Travolta was fortunate to be able to befriend his idol. In 1980, he wangled an invitation to Cagney's Beverly Hills house for a St. Patrick's Day party. The two hit it off, with Travolta even performing his dance steps from *Urban Cowboy*. He invited Cagney and wife Frances for a two-day visit to El Adobe Tajiguas, his Santa Barbara hacienda, which he had purchased after his initial success, with the trip ending up stretched to four days. "We did a lot of walking, talking about my past and his past, his viewpoint on acting and mine, and watching movies, his and mine," Travolta recalled soon afterward. "Basically, *being* with him was what I always wanted to do; I just wanted to know him." Later that year, Travolta had his *Moment by Moment* failure in mind when he

observed, "It's so important for me to talk to people like Jimmy Cagney. They're giving me hope because they've gone through the same thing."

Also in 1980, Cagney was one of the year's Kennedy Center honorees, along with Leonard Bernstein, Agnes De Mille, Lynn Fontanne, and Leontyne Price. Tributes were offered Cagney by Mikhail Baryshnikov, Pat O'Brien—and Travolta. O'Brien introduced Travolta by declaring, "You know, there's a lad here tonight for whom [Cagney] has great expectations. And I trust and I know, having met the boy, that Jimmy will be a prophet . . ." Travolta, garbed in tuxedo and bow tie, told the audience:

> When I was about five years old on, there was a television program in New York City called *The Million Dollar Movie*. Now, you could see a Cagney movie maybe seven or eight times a year, but the difference was you could see it five times a day, five days a week. And if *Yankee Doodle Dandy* was on, you would find me in front of the television set five days a week, five times a day. And I would be trying the poses and singing the songs—even

Travolta was delighted to have befriended Cagney. Along with Mikhail Baryshnikov and Pat O'Brien, Travolta offered a tribute to Cagney, a Kennedy Center honoree.

James Cagney, Travolta's all-time favorite screen legend, as he appears in *Yankee Doodle Dandy*, Travolta's all-time favorite movie.

that walk up the wall that Mr. Cagney does, I used to try that and there'd be footprints all over the house and my mother would get furious.

But finally my mother took advantage of the situation. I wasn't a well-behaved child. I think I was a discipline problem. In order to get me to do things like behave and do errands and chores, she'd pretend that Cagney was on the phone. And she'd say, 'Okay, Cagney says, brush your teeth! Okay, Cagney says, clean your room . . .' Whatever Cagney said went . . .

Twenty years later, I was fortunate to get to meet Mr. Cagney and know him, and I think I can honestly say that I'm a friend. He still breaks my heart and inspires me at the same time. . . .

Twenty-Three

More Starring Roles

White Man's Burden (1995)

Rysher Entertainment/Savoy Pictures. Director-Screenplay: Desmond Nakano. Producer: Lawrence Bender. Cinematographer: Willy Kurant Music: Howard Shore. Editor: Nancy Richardson. CAST: John Travolta *(Louis Pinnock)*, Harry Belafonte *(Thaddeus Thomas)*, Kelly Lynch *(Marsha Pinnock)*, Margaret Avery *(Megan Thomas)*, Tom Bower *(Stanley)*, Carrie Snodgress *(Josene)*, Andrew Lawrence *(Donnie)*, Bumper Robinson *(Martin)*, Tom Wright *(Lionel)*, Sheryl Lee Ralph *(Roberta)*, Judith Drake *(Dorothy)*, Robert Gossett *(John)*, Wesley Thompson *(Williams)*, Tom Nolan *(Johansson)*, Willie C. Carpenter *(Marcus)*, Michael Beach *(Policeman no. 1 Outside Bar)*, Lee Duncan *(Policeman no. 2 Outside Bar)*, Lawrence Bender *(Bar Patron no. 1)*. 89 minutes. Rated: R.

Prior to filming *Get Shorty*, Travolta made *White Man's Burden*, a low-budget, independently produced feature directed by first-timer Desmond Nakano, a Tarantino buddy. In fact, it was Tarantino who brought Nakano's script to Travolta. "I just thought this was a good role and a really good script," the actor explained, just as the film was set to open. "I don't know if race is the most important issue in America, but it is certainly one of the most important, and I liked that the script was addressing it."

Agreeing to star in *White Man's Burden* was a career move strikingly similar to the one Travolta had made almost two decades earlier regarding *Moment by Moment*, in that his character would veer markedly from the ones which had earned him success. Just as *Moment by Moment* was meant to be a serious statement on feminism, a departure from the essentially escapist nature of *Saturday Night Fever* and *Grease*, *White Man's Burden* is a sobering, politically loaded allegory that is far removed from the hip satire of *Pulp Fiction* and *Get Shorty*.

White Man's Burden is the story of Louis Pinnock (Travolta), who exists in a society in which the position of blacks and whites has been switched. Blacks have the seats at the dinner table. Whites are the servants. Blacks live the lush life in high-toned neighborhoods. Whites are

131

Travolta as Louis Pinnock, the troubled lead character in *White Man's Burden*.

consigned to dreary, crime-ridden ghettos. Blacks own the factories. Whites work the assembly lines and struggle to pay their bills. Blacks are refined. Whites are ill-educated. Black cops harass white citizens. Blacks dominate the airwaves. The "poor people" to whom blacks patronizingly refer, and who in the past have "burned down their community" and presently are "beyond being helped," are white. A black mother is taken aback when her son brings home a white girl, a girl of the lower classes. Regarding the manner in which his race is perceived by blacks, a white man observes, "At night they think we all look like ghosts."

Finally, and most specific to the scenario of *White Man's Burden*, blacks like Thaddeus Thomas (Harry Belafonte), owner of the factory where Pinnock works, hold the power. Whites like Pinnock are powerless, and defenseless.

Pinnock may be inarticulate, but he is a nice guy who diligently works at his job and hopes for a promotion. He also is a good husband and loving father. (His son, Donnie, is played by Andrew Lawrence, kid

brother of Joey.) However, a swift chain of events—occurring after Pinnock accidently sees Thomas's wife naked while delivering a package to his estate—leaves Pinnock unemployed, battered by some overly zealous cops, and cruelly evicted from his home. Pinnock only can find jobs which pay minimum wage. They are the kind he might have had as a teenager, and they will not allow him to support his family. His sense of pride and self-worth have been systematically stripped from him. Facing a wall of bureaucracy and growing increasingly desperate, Pinnock abducts Thomas and demands to be paid the money he feels is owed him for lost wages. But this act escalates into tragedy: Pinnock is gunned down by the police after Thomas is felled by what appears to be a heart attack, and the kidnapper attempts to save his victim's life.

White Man's Burden is an explosive film. It makes viewers of both races feel uneasy because it deals in uncomfortable truths regarding racism, classism, and the loss of manhood and self-respect. Pinnock's anger is justified, given the manner in which he is victimized. The question of what he is supposed to do with his feelings is indeed provocative. When Thomas patronizingly tells Pinnock to solve his problem by find-

Pinnock and Thaddeus Thomas (Harry Belafonte), during the tragic finale of *White Man's Burden*.

ing himself another job, he shows an appalling lack of understanding of the reality of Pinnock's situation.

However, the film is seriously flawed, in that its scenario makes excuses for soaring crime rates among the poor. If a poor person commits a robbery, the film seems to say, it is only because he is desperate, he cannot find a decent job, he has no alternative. Plus, that person will be stealing only what he feels is rightfully his. These generalizations are, to say the least, naive. The scenario does not address the issue of personal responsibility. Pinnock may have been wronged by an impersonal society, but it is nevertheless wrong for him to kidnap Thomas.

Another major flaw is the extreme depiction of all blacks as haves and all whites as have-nots. The inference is that the opposite holds true in contemporary American society. Such an observation might have been correct in the 1950s or earlier. But today, this is not the case. At one point, Pinnock's son channel-clicks on his television set, and the only faces he sees are black ones. Today, television is a highly integrated medium, populated by blacks, Hispanics, and Orientals as well as whites.

While *White Man's Burden* received decidedly mixed reviews, none of the film's faults were attributed to Travolta. Stephen Holden, reviewing the film in the *New York Times*, called it "a dull but well-meaning essay on race relations," while noting that "Travolta creates a sympathetic portrait of a man who becomes unstrung."

Travolta, complete with dyed-red hair and the conspicuous middle-aged spread that is the appropriate physical baggage for a man like Pinnock, actually offers a performance that is much more than sympathetic. He captures Pinnock's growing rage with appropriate ferocity, and his acting is as forceful as his work in *Pulp Fiction* and *Get Shorty*.

Broken Arrow (1996)

Twentieth Century-Fox. Director: John Woo. Producers: Mark Gordon, Bill Badalato, and Terence Chang. Screenplay: Graham Yost. Cinematographer: Peter Levy. Music: Hans Zimmer. Editors: John Wright, Steve Mirkovich, and Joe Hutshing. CAST: John Travolta *(Vic Deakins)*, Christian Slater *(Riley Hale)*, Samantha Mathis *(Terry Carmichael)*, Delroy Lindo *(Col. Max Wilkins)*, Frank Whaley *(Giles Prentice)*, Bob Gunton *(Pritchett)*, Howie Long *(Kelly)*, Jack Thompson *(Chairman, Joint Chiefs of Staff)*, Kurtwood Smith *(Secretary of Defense)*, Vondie Curtis-Hall *(Lt. Col. Sam Rhodes)*. 108 minutes. Rated: R.

Travolta (center), surrounded by co-star Christian Slater (left) and director John Woo (right), on the set of *Broken Arrow*.

Broken Arrow is Travolta's first out-and-out action movie (if you don't count the final section of *Chains of Gold*). In it, he plays his first villain since *Carrie*, made two decades earlier. Travolta's character, Air Force Maj. Vic Deakins, is as rugged and hearty as Vincent Vega is pasty-faced and in need of a health-club membership.

Deakins is a twenty-year veteran aviator who has flown "a hundred missions in the Gulf." Currently he is piloting a B-3 Stealth bomber, and is the superior officer of, and mentor to, his younger copilot, Capt. Riley Hale (Christian Slater). As the film opens, Deakins and Hale are shown to be friendly rivals who spar in a boxing ring, with the former giving the latter a lesson in pugilism. No sooner are they airborne, soaring over Monument Valley with their aircraft loaded with two nuclear warheads, when Deakins attempts to kill Hale by ejecting him from the jet. This is the first step shown in a diabolical scenario in which Deakins and his band of rogues will steal the "live nukes" and blackmail the United States government for $250 million.

Hale, of course, survives the ordeal, and with the able assistance of Terry Carmichael (Samantha Mathis), a park ranger who happens upon him in the Utah desert, he employs his ingenuity to thwart Deakins's scheme.

In some ways, the true star of *Broken Arrow* is director John Woo. The film is a nonstop roller coaster ride in which narrative coherence is subordinate to Woo's trademarks: eye-poppingly vivid action sequences set within a scenario reflecting allegiance versus betrayal. The story Woo tells is the age-old one of greed, and what some people will go through to satisfy it. Yet there is plenty of state-of-the-art technology employed to thrill audiences. Lots of gadgetry is paraded across the screen, along with endless explosions, gun battles and narrow escapes, stunts and special effects. While the specifics of Deakins's scheme and Hale's and Carmichael's heroics are illogical, and as credible as the scenario of a Road Runner cartoon, they nonetheless are amusing and exciting to watch.

Travolta as villainous Vic Deakins in *Broken Arrow.*

Deakins threatens to explode bomb number two.

Travolta plays Deakins with panache, making him much more than a stock villain. The major is a cocksure psycho who struts across the screen, with an ego the size of his Stealth bomber. Travolta contorts his face, grates his teeth, and insidiously smiles as he expresses Deakins's knavery. He has some dazzling one-liners, which he delivers with zeal. "I say, goddamn, what a rush!" he squeals after one of the bombs explodes underground, resulting in the earth rippling as if it were a wave on the ocean. In the climactic sequence, Deakins and Hale are reunited, and are immersed in mortal combat with the last bomb about to go off. "You're out of your mind!" Hale blurts out to his ex-friend. Deakins maniacally smiles and responds, "Ain't it cool!"

"I hope I've made him fun to watch," Travolta observed of Deakins, before the film opened. Obviously, he is enjoying playing the role, and he is indeed fun to watch, every second he is on screen. As was *Get Shorty*, *Broken Arrow* was an immediate audience favorite. In its first week of release, it earned $15.6 million, ranking number one at the box office.

Phenomenon (1996)

Touchstone Pictures. Director: Jon Turteltaub. Producers: Barbara Boyle and Michael Taylor. Screenplay: Gerald DiPego. Cinematographer: Phedon Papamichael. Music: Thomas Newman. Executive Soundtrack Producer: Robbie Robertson. Editor: Bruce

Green. Cast: John Travolta *(George Malley)*, Kyra Sedgwick *(Lace Pennamin)*, Forest Whitaker *(Nate Pope)*, Robert Duvall *(Doc)*, Jeffrey DeMunn *(Professor Ringold)*, Richard Kiley *(Dr. Wellin)*, Brent Spiner *(Niedorf)*, Vyto Ruginis *(Ted Rhome)*, Bruce Young *(Jack Hatch)*, Michael Milhoan *(Jimmy)*, Sean O'Bryan *(Banes)*, David Gallagher *(Al)*, Ashley Buccille *(Glory)*, Tony Genaro *(Tito)*, Elisabeth Nunziato *(Ella)*, Mark Valim *(Alberto)*, Troy Evans *(Roger)*, Ellen Geer *(Bonnie)*, James Keane *(Pete)*, Susan Merson *(Marge)*, James Cotton *(Cal)*.
117 minutes. Rated: PG.

With *Phenomenon*, a combination science fiction fantasy/love story/*Forrest Gump* variation, Travolta showed that his villainous role in *Broken Arrow* was a career aberration. In fact, this is the first film in his "second" career in which he plays a character who is not in one way or another antisocial. His George Malley may be like Louis Pinnock in that he is solidly blue-collar, but he does not feel compelled to become a kidnapper in order to rise above the crush of humanity. Still, Malley and Pinnock are alike in that they are ordinary men who find themselves in extraordinary situations.

George Malley is an otherwise average, all-around nice guy who runs an auto repair shop in the small Northern California town in which he has resided all his life. On his thirty-seventh birthday, he notices a mysterious bright light in the sky which literally knocks him off his feet. Miraculously, this nondescript man finds that he has instantly become a modern-era Einstein. For no logical reason he cannot stop reading, and he begins absorbing two to four books a day. He becomes an instant whiz at chess. He finds that he can speak fluent Spanish, and then masters Portuguese in twenty minutes. He transforms pig manure into fuel. He concocts an organic fertilizer that produces tomatoes the size of softballs. He feels the presence of ultra-low-frequency sound waves, allowing him to predict an oncoming earthquake. He becomes "magnetic": tools, books and pencils take on lives of their own when they come near his fingertips.

Phenomenon: Is that the hum of the carburetor in Lace's (Kyra Sedgwick) pick-up truck, or is it the stepped-up beat of auto mechanic George Malley's heart? © Touchstone Pictures.

But most significantly, he philosophizes on the essence and meaning of life. Even as his new-found abilities are second-guessed, and some come to view him as if he is a "green bug," he expounds eloquently on human potential and the beauty of the human spirit.

Malley has become a "phenomenon," albeit one who is destined to shine brightly but ever-so-briefly. Here is where the scenario veers perilously into "disease of the week" territory: a CAT-SCAN reveals that his brain cells are more active than anyone ever tested—but, at the same time, he has an inoperable brain tumor. He only has weeks to live. Perhaps even days.

Despite this dire turn of events, *Phenomenon* is designed as a populist crowd-pleaser. Its scenario puts forth a point-of-view that has become fashionable in mid-1990s Hollywood films: power structures are inherently evil, and are not to be trusted because they regard the individual as expendable. As word spreads of Malley's brilliance, the "authorities" summarily regard him with suspicion. The FBI puts him under surveillance, and he is considered a "security risk." Medical science wants him to become a human guinea pig. When he chooses not to accommo-

date the request of a manipulative medico, he is robbed of his freedom and kept prisoner in his hospital room—even though he has literally days to live.

The film's point-of-view is that the individual only can trust his friends and family: the other individuals to whom he is close. And he will find happiness only if he relates to real people, not the celebrities force-fed the public by the media. Nate (Forest Whitaker), Malley's best friend, fixates on Diana Ross. Perhaps he would spend his entire life dreaming that Diana will "touch him in the morning," but then George plays cupid by setting him up with a Portuguese woman who will become Nate's real-life "angel," and real-life true love.

George Malley is an unusual role for Travolta—indeed, it is the antithesis of his on- and off-screen persona—in that he is a guy who has been unable to get the girl. But not for long. At first, Lace (Kyra Sedgwick), the new-in-town divorcee on whom he has a crush, is unresponsive. To her, he is just another insincere guy who will love her and then leave her. But Malley is oh, so sweet. In *Look Who's Talking* fash-

A newly-enlightened George Malley (Travolta) points the way to his friend Doc (Robert Duvall) in *Phenomenon*. © Touchstone Pictures.

ion, he is attentive to Lace's two children, winning them over before melting away her iciness. Soon, she gazes lovingly at him. After escaping his hospital confinement, Malley makes his way to Lace's house to die. He does just that, after they make love for the first time.

Malley is an Everyman who is touched by greatness, and Travolta's performance is endearing and wholly believable. He makes the character ingratiating, and touchingly human. Travolta is perfectly cast in *Phenomenon*, just as he was perfectly cast as Vic Deakins and Chili Palmer, Louis Pinnock and Vincent Vega.

The film did nothing to taint Travolta's new-found popularity. It opened over the July 4 holiday, taking in $16.2 million in its first weekend in release. *Phenomenon* ranked a solid number three in earnings for the period, behind *Independence Day* ($50.2 million) and *The Nutty Professor* ($17.5 million).

Future Projects

In February, 1996, Travolta began filming *Michael*, directed and co-scripted by Nora Ephron, about a besotted archangel. His costars were William Hurt and Andie MacDowell, and the film is scheduled for a

Christmas, 1996 release.

Upon completing *Michael*, Travolta's next project was supposed to have been *The Double*, adapted from a work by Dostoyevsky, directed by Roman Polanski and costarring John Goodman and Isabelle Adjani. His role was to have been an American accountant in Paris who is convinced a lookalike has taken his identity. However, on June 2, 1996, three days into rehearsal and two weeks before the on-location shooting was to begin, Travolta walked off the set.

Mandalay Entertainment, the film's production company, announced that he had left because his son, Jett, had become ill. The four-year-old had water behind his eardrums, which needed to be drained, and Travolta—a doting and loving dad who is no stereotypical absentee Hollywood father—insisted on returning to Los Angeles. But then word emerged that he had been feuding with Polanski over the film's script, and the filmmaker's vision for the work. Mandalay filed a breach-of-contract lawsuit in Los Angeles Superior Court, claiming that Travolta had attempted to take control of the project. According to the suit, the actor "simply changed his mind about doing the Picture because his ego had been bruised by Polanski's legitimate efforts to direct Travolta's performance during the rehearsal period."

Travolta's camp claimed that it was within his jurisdiction to approve the screenplay, and offer input regarding the manner in which his character would be played. In fact, Travolta maintained that the script was now markedly different from the one he had seen a year-and-a-half before, when he okayed the project. Supposedly, approximately one-fifth of it had been altered. Additionally, Polanski had decided that he wanted Travolta to play his role in a broad comic manner, an approach with which the actor was completely uncomfortable. Travolta felt that, with the rules of the game so altered, he would be unable to do his best work.

Steve Martin was announced as Travolta's replacement. However, Mandalay opted to put off the project just as shooting was set to begin. The company issued a statement that the film's "producers and Steve Martin all feel that it is in the best interest of the project to postpone photography. It became evident after John Travolta's eleventh-hour departure that a delay was necessary because of the scheduling needs of the other actors and key crew, the retooling of the script to adapt the role for Steve Martin, and the overall production realities of trying to start this picture under such constraints."

Just as *The Double* was postponed, Travolta signed to star in *Mad City*, a Constantin Costa-Gavras-directed drama. It also had been announced that he would appear in *Face Off*, about a detective who goes undercover after surgically switching faces with a terrorist. Travolta would be cast opposite Nicolas Cage, the Best Actor Oscar–winner for *Leaving Las Vegas*, and his director would be John Woo. A slew of other potential projects were cited in the press. Perhaps the most intriguing: a biography of controversial Italian-American crooner Jimmy Roselli, who was both admired and abhorred by organized crime (which was unable to regulate his career). Others were *She's De Lovely*, scripted by the late John Cassavetes and directed by his son Nick, in which Travolta would appear opposite Sean Penn and Robin Wright; *Lady Takes a Flyer*, costarring Sharon Stone; and *Dark Horse*, a political thriller. Travolta also had been developing two science fiction/fantasy-oriented projects based on *Fear* and *Battlefield Earth*, stories authored by Scientology founding father L. Ron Hubbard.

Travolta was to have been paid a whopping $17 million for *The Double*. Prior to *Pulp Fiction*, his highest salary on a picture was $3 million. "I think I did that about five different times," he once remarked. As per his "has-been" status, he was paid a lowly $150,000 for *Pulp Fiction*—mere pocket change for a movie star. He reportedly lost money on the deal, as he financed the relocation of his family to Los Angeles for the shoot.

However, Travolta's *Get Shorty* salary was a healthy $5 million, and he earned $7 million for *Broken Arrow*, between $8 and $9 million for *Phenomenon*, and upwards of $10 to $11 million for *Michael*. His *Get Shorty* contract reportedly included a provision whereby he earned a $750,000 bonus for copping an Oscar nomination for *Pulp Fiction*.

In November 1995, *Variety*—in an article headlined TRAVOLTA IN LINE TO REWRITE SUPERSTAR SALARY SCALE—related how the actor was set to become the movies' first $21 million man. Jim Carrey recently had signed to star in *The Cable Guy* for $20 million. Sylvester Stallone reportedly had inked a $60 million, three-picture deal with Universal. Jonathan D. Krane, Travolta's manager, and Fred Westheimer, his agent, were convinced that their star was ready to one-up Carrey and Stallone. "John's a sweet guy, and hardly a money-grubbing star," Krane told *Variety*. "The last factor in making decisions for us is price. He'll only do a movie because it's a good movie." Yet Krane went on to describe $21 million as Travolta's "true value," adding that he and Westheimer felt that "he deserves it and we've gotten feedback from studios saying they will pay that price. What we don't want is for him to be labeled as a guy who won't do a job for less."

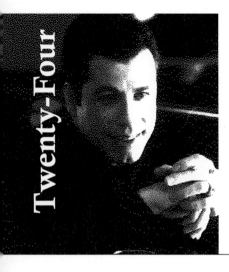

Twenty-Four

Travolta Cool

When Travolta is being John Travolta, he professes that he is anything but hip.

"The truth is I don't feel cool at all," he told *Tonight Show* host Jay Leno. "I feel cool in the characters that I play on the screen. In life, I feel like a goofball." He went on to relate how, at age eighteen, he bragged to friends that he had done well at an audition and promptly broke his nose after diving into the shallow end of a swimming pool. More recently, he decided to drive around Hollywood in a red Jaguar. He felt like being "very full of myself," so he took the top down and began making up his own words to the theme song of *A Man and a Woman*: "Oh, I am such a great movie star, such a great movie star, and everybody's looking at me now, looking at me now." The Jaguar promptly broke down—right in the middle of a busy section of Sunset Boulevard.

On-screen, Travolta is irrefutably cool. In most of his films, from the heights of *Saturday Night Fever* and *Pulp Fiction* to the dregs of his direct-to-video potboilers, Travolta appears on-screen with cigarette in hand. Back in the days when the Production Code ruled Hollywood and on-screen sex was taboo, lighting up a Lucky Strike was a sure sign of sexual attraction between a man and a woman. Aside from the fact that puffing on them, and filling up your lungs with nicotine, has been proven to rot your insides and shorten your life, the image of a cigarette dangling from the lips of a rugged actor remains undeniably sexy.

While Travolta's career has encompassed a time in which sex, and graphic sexual references, are common in movies, cigarettes never-theless have become synonymous with his appeal. Indeed, given the number of times Travolta has lit up in his movies, he easily might be named his era's tobacco industry pinup boy.

In *Saturday Night Fever*, Travolta begins his long-standing on-screen affiliation with cigarette smoking. Tony Manero lights one up the first time he enters 2001 Odyssey. As he sits in a diner and chats with

(*Opposite*) Despite their unhealthi-ness, cigarettes have been inexorably linked to the Travolta-cool mystique, and throughout his career the actor has been a walking ad for the tobacco industry. Early into his fame, he is posed in his *Saturday Night Fever* disco outfit, cigarette in hand.

Stephanie, he lights up another. These acts would be insignificant, if not
for the fact that Travolta very conspicuously smokes cigarettes in a number of subsequent screen roles.

Throughout *Grease*, a cigarette is never far from Travolta's lips.
The first time he is seen on-screen in *Blow Out*, he is smoking. Scott
Barnes, his character in *Chains of Gold*, is an amalgam of the John
Travolta screen persona of old. In his initial appearance in the movie, he
talks tough—and smokes a cigarette. Throughout the course of the film,
the character chain smokes. In *Shout*, as Travolta's character, rock 'n'
roll fugitive Jack Cabe, lights up a cigarette, he is meant to recall Tony
Manero and Danny Zuko.

It is not surprising when James, Travolta's character in *Look
Who's Talking*, smokes. The difference here is that he now is in the company of the infant Mikey. At one point, James begins lighting up a cigarette, which Kirstie Alley's Mollie grabs away from him. "Don't smoke
that around my baby," she admonishes.

Travolta conspicuously smokes in *Pulp Fiction*. As Vincent Vega
sits down to dine with Mia at Jack Rabbit Slim's, he even rolls his own.
In a prominent shot of Travolta in one of the *Broken Arrow* screen trail-

John
TRAVOLTA

公開前から日本でもすごい人気です。「サタデー・ナイト・フィーバー」の好演でアカデミー賞の候補にまで選ばれたジョン・トラボルタ。青春スターのトップを走って、キャリアの上り坂はまだまだ続きます。

ers, the actor is seen lighting up a cigarette. "John Woo wanted me dressed well and smoking a certain kind of cigarette," he declared, as the film was set to open.

Indeed, the first shot of Travolta after the film's opening boxing sequence is of his hand. Between his fingers is a cigarette, which he smoothly guides toward his lips. Throughout the rest of the film, amid the nonstop action, he chain-smokes.

Additionally, Travolta—à la Brando, Dean, and other individualistic, rebel-hero actors—often wears T-shirts on screen. He goes collar-less not just in the films made when he was young and lithe but also in those in which his middle-age paunch is apparent.

Travolta-cool for the Asian market.

In his first appearance in the premiere episode of *Welcome Back, Kotter*, Travolta is garbed in a red T-shirt (along with jeans and a dungaree jacket). After his sojourn into polyester for *Saturday Night Fever*, he again is T-shirted in *Grease*. And the characters he plays in the films that followed often wear T-shirts. When social worker Scott Barnes, in *Chains of Gold*, is away from his office, he wears them: first a gray one, then a white one. Black is the color of Jack Cabe's T-shirts in *Shout*. In the first *Look Who's Talking* film, Travolta's James is garbed in a red T-shirt when he initially appears on screen. When James first visits Mollie and Mikey, he wears a black T-shirt. Later on, he wears a white one, and a green one.

Cigarettes and T-shirts, T-shirts and cigarettes. Both are intrinsic parts of Travolta's supercool, super-hip screen image.

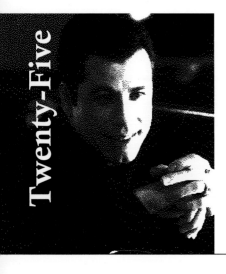

Twenty-Five

Aborted Projects

Way back when he was an unknown, Travolta unsuccessfully auditioned for a supporting role in the 1973 feature *The Last Detail*. The character, Meadows, was a kleptomaniacal sailor being transported to the brig. His costar would have been Jack Nicholson. Randy Quaid was chosen instead, and went on to win an Oscar nomination. Had Travolta been cast, his career surely would have taken a different path. However, two years later, the casting agent of *The Last Detail* called him in to read for the part of Vinnie Barbarino.

Prior to auditioning for *Welcome Back, Kotter*, Travolta nixed a role in the Broadway production of Terence McNally's *The Ritz*—despite a weekly salary of $750. Had he accepted it, he might have ended up becoming his generation's Len Cariou or John McMartin.

Travolta originally had planned to shorten his summer theater run in *Bus Stop* to take a movie role. Because of a scheduling conflict, the powers-that-be at *Welcome Back, Kotter* vetoed the move, and Travolta lost the part. The film was Terrence Malick's *Days of Heaven*, released in 1978. His character would have been Bill, a turn-of-the-twentieth-century steel mill worker who is fired from his job, and who sets out with his girlfriend and kid sister to find employment in the midwest wheatfields. Travolta reportedly believed that *Days of Heaven* would have transformed him into the new Jack Nicholson. But the part was played by Richard Gere.

A year later, Travolta was cast in *American Gigolo*, playing a slimy, hardened variation of *Saturday Night Fever*'s Tony Manero and *Moment by Moment*'s Strip: Julian, a Beverly Hills stud-for-hire. Paul Schrader, the film's director, wanted Travolta because "his sexual electricity is a given. With many other actors, you would have to spend half the movie imbuing them with sexual appeal."

Three weeks before he was to begin shooting *American Gigolo*, Travolta backed out of the project. His mother had died. *Moment By Moment* had opened to dreadful reviews. He allegedly was having cre-

Travolta auditioned for, but failed to win, the role of a young sailor being escorted to the brig in *The Last Detail.* Randy Quaid (at left, with Otis Young and Jack Nicholson) got the role, and received a Best Supporting Actor Academy Award nomination.

ative differences with Schrader. Eric Roberts, Tom Berenger, and Christopher Reeve were cited as possible replacements. However, the actor who eventually played Julian was . . . Richard Gere.

In the early 1980s, Travolta turned down the starring role in *An Officer and a Gentleman*, as a maverick who goes into training in Naval Officer Candidate School. The part had been written for him, and he would have been reteamed with Debra Winger, his *Urban Cowboy* costar. Instead, he chose to enroll in American Airlines jet pilot training school. The actor who went on to star in the film was . . . Richard Gere.

In 1980, it was announced that Travolta would sign on to star in the screen version of the record-breaking Broadway musical *A Chorus Line*. The story, about the rigors of a group of Broadway gypsies as they audition for a musical, would have been a natural extension of *Saturday Night Fever*. Travolta wanted to work on the film with James Bridges, who had just directed him in *Urban Cowboy*. His salary would have been $5 million, one-fourth of the film's projected budget. Additionally, the scenario would have been reworked to create a juicier role for Travolta. "It would be a dynamite vehicle for me," he declared. "Obviously it would have to be revamped, but I wouldn't change it so that all the other parts got lost. It would still, more or less, remain an ensemble piece."

At the time, directors Michael Bennett (the force behind the stage show), Mike Nichols, and Sidney Lumet, and screenwriters Joel Schumacher and Bo Goldman, already had worked on the project's pre-

Travolta was set to play the role of a male prostitute in *American Gigolo*, but backed out in favor of Richard Gere. In the film, Gere was handsomely clad in Giorgio Armani suits, which went on to become hugely popular. Had he appeared in the film, Travolta would have been responsible for initiating yet another fashion trend, after *Saturday Night Fever's* polyester and *Urban Cowboy's* western chic.

production. Mikhail Baryshnikov had been mentioned as a possible costar. Another piece of scuttlebut had Travolta and Baryshnikov linking up for a dance-related project to be directed by Milos Forman.

But none came to fruition. *A Chorus Line* finally made it to movie screens in 1985, directed by Richard Attenborough and starring Michael Douglas as the show's director and a cast of lesser-knowns as the dancers. The results were disappointing, a limp and forgettable adaptation of a stunning Broadway show. One can only wonder what it might have been with the participation of Travolta.

In 1983, Travolta very much wanted to star in *Mass Appeal*, the screen version of Bill C. Davis's Broadway play. His role would have been Mark Dolson, a spunky young seminarian who attacks the methodology and jars the complacency of Father Farley, a well-liked parish priest. But Travolta's salary requirement was $3 million, which then was his standard fee per picture, and the film was budgeted at only $6 million. "He wanted to do it; we wanted him for it—but we couldn't get together on salary," explained David Foster, the film's producer.

Zeljko Ivanek, an actor unknown to movies, who had been appearing on Broadway in *Brighton Beach Memoirs*, won the role of Mark Dolson; Father Farley was played by Jack Lemmon.

In 1984, Travolta was offered, and wanted to accept, the male lead in *Splash*, as a man who becomes romantically involved with a mermaid. However, Michael Ovitz, who then was his agent, persuaded him

Travolta might have been one of the Broadway gypsies auditioning for *A Chorus Line*.

to decline, because Warren Beatty was planning to shoot a movie with a similar theme. Beatty's film was never made, while *Splash* ended up bringing instant screen stardom to Tom Hanks.

Before he played Barbarino (and, for that matter, before he appeared on Broadway in *Over Here!*), Travolta and Robby Benson were finalists for the part of Michael Corleone's son in *The Godfather, Part II*. Benson won the role, which ended up on the cutting room floor. As early as 1978, it was reported that Travolta definitely would appear in *The Godfather, Part III*, also playing Corleone's son. Filming would not begin until after he completed *Moment by Moment*, *American Gigolo*, and *Prince of the City*. But *The Godfather III* was not made at that time. Neither did Travolta appear in *Prince of the City*, a based-on-fact drama which starred Treat Williams as a New York City cop who is victimized after exposing corruption in his unit.

Just after the out-of-left-field success of *Saturday Night Fever*, reports circulated that Travolta had nixed starring in a sequel, to be titled *Saturday Night Fever II*. But in 1983, after having suffered career setbacks, he appeared in *Staying Alive*. At the time, Travolta and

Sylvester Stallone expressed interest in working together in *The Godfather, Part III*. When Francis Coppola did make the film in 1990, two of the major new characters were Vincent Mancini, Michael Corleone's hot-tempered nephew, and Joey Zasa, a brutal hoodlum who rivals the Corleone clan. Travolta and Stallone might have been cast in these roles. Instead, they were played by Andy Garcia and Joe Mantegna.

Over the years, dozens of proposed Travolta projects were announced in the press. A slew came directly after *Saturday Night Fever*. In addition to *Saturday Night Fever II*, one report had him starring as Michael Brody, a young man who back in the 1970s earned his fifteen minutes of fame by handing out thousands of dollars to strangers on the New York City streets.

Another had Travolta featured in the screen version of the Broadway musical *Promises, Promises*, cast opposite Linda Ronstadt. The show was based on *The Apartment*, Billy Wilder's Oscar-winner about an ambitious young executive who hopes to ascend the corporate latter by lending his bachelor flat to his superiors, and who eventually falls in love with his boss's mistress.

In 1978, Travolta and his manager, Bob LeMond, purchased the screen rights to Anne Rice's *Interview With the Vampire*. Travolta was to have starred as Lestadt, and shooting was announced for New Orleans, San Francisco, and New York, beginning in June 1979. Of course, *Interview With the Vampire* was not made until 1994, with Tom Cruise as Lestadt. Travolta also reported that James Ivory had desired to cast him in *Slaves of New York*, and Robert Altman considered him for the role of Griffin Mill, the hotshot young movie mogul in *The Player*.

In 1984, gossip columnist Liz Smith noted that Travolta soon would be making his directorial debut in a film to be titled *Greenwich*, "about a rags-to-riches family in Connecticut." In 1985, Travolta observed, "It's about people who were born with money and have to

adjust to complete poverty afterwards and how unpleasant it is for them." *Greenwich* was scheduled to have been filmed that fall, but the project fell apart.

Around that time, Travolta was contemplating starring in *Fire*, a Jim Morrison biography, to be directed by Brian De Palma and choreographed by Jeffrey Hornaday. Nothing came of that; in 1991, Oliver Stone told Morrison's story in *The Doors*, starring Val Kilmer. Also in the mid-1980s, Travolta and Whoopi Goldberg spent a year developing a comedy, to be produced by Cannon Films. He reported that they could not come up with an appropriate script, and so the project was abandoned.

Most intriguing of all, when *Saturday Night Fever* was the rage, Liz Smith reported that another "possibility" for Travolta was a role in a film created for him and Fred Astaire. "Hollywood's greatest dancer thinks Travolta is just sensational," wrote the gossip columnist, "and there is talk that as a young-old duet, they might dream up something together where they could pay tribute to the great Terpsichore."

After his success in *Pulp Fiction*, Travolta's name again was linked to an assortment of film projects. "From the moment the film was seen at Cannes, [industry] people have been coming to John with offers," reported Jonathan D. Krane, the producer of several of Travolta's films, who also had become the actor's manager.

Travolta turned down the starring role, eventually played by Richard Gere, in *An Officer and A Gentleman*. His costar would have been Debra Winger, his *Urban Cowboy* leading lady.

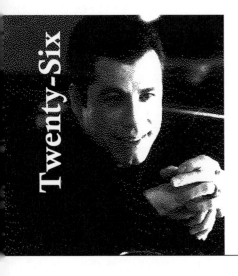

Twenty-Six

And the Winner Is . . .

In 1978, in the wake of *Saturday Night Fever* and *Grease*, a Reuters News Agency survey cited Travolta and Jane Fonda as the year's most popular film stars. The poll covered fifty-nine countries across the globe, excluding the United States and Canada. As a result, Travolta and Fonda won World Film Favorites Awards, presented during the Golden Globe Awards ceremony held in January 1979.

Also in 1978, Travolta was ranked number two on the list of Top Box-Office Stars, based on a Quigley Publications poll of movie exhibitors. Ranking ahead of him was Burt Reynolds. He was followed by Richard Dreyfuss, Warren Beatty, Clint Eastwood, Woody Allen, Diane Keaton, Jane Fonda, Peter Sellers, and Barbra Streisand. The following year, he slid to seventh place, and in 1980 moved up to sixth. In both those years, Reynolds remained solidly entrenched as number one. Travolta was off the roll for the next two years, but was listed in fifth place for 1983. By that time, Eastwood had replaced Reynolds in the number-one slot.

Among Travolta's other awards and citations:

- Academy Award nomination, *Saturday Night Fever*

- Golden Globe nomination, *Saturday Night Fever*

- Best Actor, National Board of Review, *Saturday Night Fever*

- Academy Award nomination, *Pulp Fiction*

- Golden Globe nomination, *Pulp Fiction*

- Screen Actors Guild nomination, *Pulp Fiction*

- Best Actor, Los Angeles Film Critics Association, *Pulp Fiction*

- Best Actor, Stockholm International Film Festival, *Pulp Fiction*

- British Academy of Film and Television Awards (BAFTA) nomination, *Pulp Fiction*

- Golden Globe award, Best Performance by an Actor in a Musical or Comedy, *Get Shorty*

- Funniest Actor in a Motion Picture, American Comedy Awards, *Get Shorty*

- Billboard Award, Best New Male Vocalist, 1976

- Man of the Year, Hasty Pudding Theatricals, Harvard University, 1981

- American Image Award, Men's Fashion Association, 1982

- National Association of Theater Owners' Male Star of the Year, 1983

- Box-Office Star of the Year, Theater Owners of America, 1990

- François Truffaut Prize, 21st annual Giffoni Film Festival, 1991

- National Association of Theater Owners/ShoWest's Male Star of the Year, 1996

Travolta beams as he displays the Billboard Award he won as Best New Male Vocalist for 1976.

Over the years, Travolta has appeared as a presenter on awards shows, from announcing the Best Supporting Actress Academy Award winner of 1978 to joining Nicolas Cage and Michael Crichton in presenting Sean Connery with the Cecil B. DeMille prize for "outstanding lifetime achievement" at the 1995 Golden Globe Awards.

Back in 1978, Oscar's fiftieth anniversary, Travolta was a nominee for *Saturday Night Fever*. Bob Hope was the host that year. In his opening monologue, he quipped, "What crowds outside! . . . when I arrived here tonight, my car was surrounded by packs of screaming women clawing to get at me. If you don't believe me, just ask my driver, John Travolta." Later on, Hope added, "I think the biggest surprise of the year is young John Travolta [in] *Saturday Night Fever*. And I mean young. I have wine older than he is." Hope described *Saturday Night Fever* as "the movie [in which] John put on a great white suit and then tried to wear it out from the inside."

The comedian soon introduced Travolta, who was the evening's first presenter. A beaming Travolta walked on stage, nattily garbed in a tuxedo with a white scarf draped around his neck. As the applause faded, he declared, "Hi. Thank you. Um, I'm very proud to be a part of this fiftieth anniversary." He then read off the Best Supporting Actress nominees: Leslie Browne (for *The Turning Point*), Quinn Cummings (*The Goodbye Girl*), Melinda Dillon (*Close Encounters of the Third Kind*), Vanessa Redgrave (*Julia*), and Tuesday Weld (*Looking for Mr. Goodbar*). Travolta announced the winner as Redgrave, who went on to give her infamous "Zionist hoodlums" speech.

In 1994, just after he won his second Oscar nomination, for *Pulp Fiction*, Travolta recalled to David Letterman what it was like to be twenty-three years old and a Best Actor finalist going up against Marcello Mastroianni (for *A Special Day*), Woody Allen (*Annie Hall*), Richard

Dreyfuss (*The Goodbye Girl*), and Richard Burton (*Equus*). "That was pretty overwhelming," he said, adding, "What happened on that one was that I really didn't think I had a chance of winning because of the obvious, of being young and new. . . . [Sylvester] Stallone gave out the Best Actor award. [As he was about to announce the winner], he said, 'the young, new, heavy-weight . . .' And I'm thinking 'Young. Well, I'm young. New. Well, I'm new.' This is all going in slow motion in my head. 'Heavyweight!' And I thought, 'Well, I don't know if I'm a heavyweight, but still . . .' " Then, Stallone blurted out the winner: Richard Dreyfuss.

Back in 1978, Travolta's actress-mother Helen described herself as having, in her earlier days, been compared to Barbara Stanwyck. Therefore, it was appropriate that Travolta was selected to hand a spe-cial prize to the veteran actress at the 1982 Academy Awards. Stanwyck was among the old-timers whom Oscar had bypassed in their prime, and whom the Academy occasionally trots out for a special citation before they pass on to that great movie set in the sky.

Travolta arrived onstage with Stanwyck's statue in his hand, with "Stayin' Alive" emanating from the orchestra pit, and went on to describe her as an "actress in control. That's the very essence of Barbara Stanwyck's eminence, that hold she has on the audience. She's reality; she's professional. And when she walks across the screen it's beauty and confidence. She's always the woman she plays, and she's always herself."

A year later, Travolta was back, this time to present the award

Travolta's actress-mother Helen once explained that, in her younger days, she had been compared to Barbara Stanwyck (pictured left, with Ronald Reagan, in *Cattle Queen of Montana*). And so, at the 1982 Academy Awards, it was appropriate that Travolta was cho-sen to hand out a special statuette to Stanwyck.

Travolta also played a hood in *Get Shorty*, the success of which proved that his *Pulp Fiction* comeback was no fluke.

for Best Actor. He was introduced by Walter Matthau as a "popular young star who will add a few more degrees to our Monday night fever," and the orchestra again played "Stayin' Alive" as he came on stage. Travolta cited the nominees: Dustin Hoffman (*Tootsie*), Ben Kingsley (*Gandhi*), Jack Lemmon (*Missing*), Paul Newman (*The Verdict*), and Peter O'Toole (*My Favorite Year*). Kingsley was the winner.

Eighteen years were to pass between Travolta's *Saturday Night Fever* nomination and his one for *Pulp Fiction*. In 1995, he told Liz Smith, "You know, I actually believed after my 1977 nomination . . . that if I did a good job every year, more nominations would come my way—I thought these things were not hard to get!" David Letterman asked Travolta if he had "a lot of folks rooting" for him to win an Oscar for *Pulp Fiction*. "In all honesty," he responded, "I've never ever felt such good will and support from fans, from the industry. It's really a revelation."

In a different year, Travolta may have had his name called as Best Actor. But *Pulp Fiction* came to movie theaters just as *Forrest Gump*–mania was sweeping across America. That film dominated the Oscars, with Tom Hanks winning as Best Actor. Paul Newman (*Nobody's Fool*), Morgan Freeman (*The Shawshank Redemption*), and Nigel Hawthorne (*The Madness of King George*) joined Travolta as also-rans.

The following year, when he won his Golden Globe Award for *Get Shorty*, Travolta repeated what had become a constant refrain since the Cannes Film Festival premiere of *Pulp Fiction*. "Oh, boy," he began. "I don't know exactly what I've done to deserve the good will that I feel the public and the press and the industry have given to me recently. But I truly do appreciate it."

That good will proved not to be enough to win Travolta an Oscar nomination for *Get Shorty*. The finalists were Nicolas Cage (the eventual winner, for *Leaving Las Vegas*), Anthony Hopkins (*Nixon*), Sean Penn (*Dead Men Walking*), the late Massimo Troisi (*The Postman*), and, ironically, old adversary Richard Dreyfuss (*Mr. Holland's Opus*).

Travolta was not the only actor slighted: Michael Douglas (*The American President*), Tom Hanks (*Apollo 13*), Ian McKellen (*Richard III*), and Laurence Fishburne (*Othello*) joined him as also-rans. Still, of all the non-nominees, Travolta was the most shocking, the most inexplicable. Immediately after the conclusion of the announcements, which were broadcast live on CNN, anchor Jim Moret noted, "As usual, there are surprises . . . not only for what was on the list but for what wasn't. John Travolta was not on the list for Best Actor. . . ." After citing the failure of *Leaving Las Vegas* to win a Best Picture nod, *Rolling Stone* film critic Peter Travers told CNN's Laurin Sydney, "But the thing that really got me off my chair was the exclusion of John Travolta as Best Actor for *Get Shorty*. I think this is one of the most popular performances, the best-liked. He won the Golden Globe for it. Where is he? Do they just hate comedy?"

Almost two decades earlier, when Travolta was nominated for *Saturday Night Fever*, he brought his parents to the ceremony. His mother already was sick with the cancer that soon would kill her. After Richard Dreyfuss was declared the winner, she asked her husband, "Did he win?" The response was in the negative. But Helen Travolta was pleased. "I'm glad," she said. "I want him to have something to look forward to."

Little did she know that, so many years later, her son still would be waiting to hear his name called after the presenter of the Best Actor Oscar ritualistically blurts out those fateful words, "And the Oscar goes to. . . ."

Twenty-Seven

In the Air

After his initial celluloid success, Travolta purchased two California properties, one a simple house in Studio City and the other El Adobe Tajiguas, a $1.5 million, seventeen-acre, five-bedroom Spanish-style ranch in the hills north of Santa Barbara. He bought a 1955 Cadillac Coupe de Ville, the first of several vintage cars he has owned. He disposed of the Santa Barbara property in 1988, the Studio City house long having been sold. He also has lived in a rented house in Carmel, a stone's throw from Clint Eastwood. By the 1990s, he had purchased a home in suburban Daytona Beach, Florida, and a mansion on an island in Penobscot Bay, off the coast of Maine.

Travolta's favorite pastimes, though, have not been collecting houses and cars. He has always loved flying, so much so that he even named his firstborn Jett.

"Both flying and acting meant being out of the crowd to me," he explained in 1977. "When I was a kid in bed late at night, I'd hear the drone of planes coming out of LaGuardia. That sound was very romantic to me. I'd wish my bed were in a plane and I could look out my window and see the stars." As a child, Travolta had loved it when his father lifted him up and spun him around the room. He would ask his dad, "How far up is the sky?" and "Why can't you make me an airplane that can fly?" He was transfixed by Mars candy commercials because the bars were depicted speeding through space.

Air flight has found its way into more than one of Travolta's movies. His character in *Broken Arrow* is a Stealth bomber pilot. One of his lines—"Flying doesn't mean what it used to mean to me"—is ironic, given Travolta's passion for airplanes. During the film's production, he playfully surprised his weary coworkers by performing a real-life airborne stunt. "They'd been working so hard," he recalled, "so I did a low-level swoop over the crew and the set. They were unglued." Of the endless actors who have played pilots over the decades, Travolta is one of the rare few who actually can maneuver an aircraft across the sky.

(Opposite) The T-shirt tells the story, as Travolta smiles for the camera.

Airplanes, large and small, always have intrigued Travolta.

In *Look Who's Talking*, his role is New York City cab driver James, who soars through the skies during his off hours. At one point, he and baby Mikey visit an airplane hangar. Later on, he takes Mollie, Mikey's mother, for a spin in a jet. In the film's two sequels, James becomes a professional pilot, flying corporate jets for wealthy clients.

Occasionally his character's lack of interest in flying becomes an in-joke. At the beginning of *Perfect*, Travolta's Adam Lawrence, a *Rolling Stone* writer, remarks, "Why don't I just fly out there [from New York to Los Angeles] tonight and try to get that interview." Responds Frankie, the magazine's photographer, "I thought you hated to fly." Lawrence retorts that he doesn't mind "as long as there's no turbulence. As soon as [planes] start bouncing around I just get drunk."

The Experts features another tongue-in-cheek reference to flying. During the film's climactic sequence, the characters played by Travolta and Arye Gross find themselves in the cockpit of a taxiing plane. "Oh, I suppose you've flown one of these before," Gross remarks. "Oh yeah, sure," is Travolta's sarcastic response, before he reveals that the only thing he ever has flown is a spaceship in a video game.

Travolta and on-screen airplanes date as far back as TV's *The Boy in the Plastic Bubble*. In one scene, young Tod Lubitch holds a model jet, saying "*woosh*" as he guides it in imaginary flight. Tod is fascinated by rocket ships and space travel, and at one point even receives a visit

from astronaut Buzz Aldrin.

Around the time he starred in *Saturday Night Fever* and *Grease*, the apartment Travolta maintained in West Hollywood had dozens of model airplanes, DC-3s, British Brittanias, and Lockheed Constellations constructed by a friend and kept in an unused bedroom. But to Travolta, airplanes were much more than toys. Earlier, while appearing on Broadway in *Over Here!*, he took flying lessons at Teterboro Airport. By the mid-1970s, he had earned a license to pilot a single-engine plane. During his first phase of earning big money, he purchased a Cessna 414, which he was prohibited from flying during the span of his contract with Robert Stigwood.

In 1981, Travolta spent three weeks in intensive flight training at the American Airlines School in Texas, and then received his private jet pilot rating from the Federal Aviation Administration. To commemorate the accomplishment, he treated Nancy Allen, his *Blow Out* costar, to a New York-to-Chicago ride in his Cessna. Over the years, he has earned a total of seven different pilot licenses.

Even the most recognizable celebrities have to show up at public airports when they wish to travel. Not Travolta. Airstrips are as much an essential part of the properties he has owned as swimming pools are to Hollywood mansions. He built a private airstrip on his Santa Barbara ranch, and his subsequent homes were equipped with takeoff and land-

Despite his youth, Travolta already was an experienced pilot when he filmed *Urban Cowboy*. Here he is in Houston, where he attended the film's premiere and hoped that its success would soar him to the heights he had achieved in *Saturday Night Fever*.

ing facilities; his Florida property is located in Spruce Creek Fly-In, an exclusive flying community.

After the failure of *Perfect*, Travolta allegedly considered retiring from acting to become a commercial airline pilot.

The man loves to travel, and rarely has he spent any length of time at any one of his properties. When not tied to one locale because of a movie shoot, he is constantly on the road, criss-crossing the country from Maine to Florida, from Florida to California, and to points between. Less frequently he travels internationally, zipping off to Africa, Switzerland, Mexico, or the Caribbean.

Over the years, Travolta has owned other jets and propeller planes, including a reconditioned commercial DC-3, an AirCoupe, a Lockheed JetStar 731, a Constellation, a Learjet, a vintage Vampire British fighter, and a Gulfstream Two executive jet. In 1991, he piloted the Lear to Camden, North Carolina, to pick up Ron Zupanzic, his executive aide, and Zupanzic's ten-month-old son (who is Travolta's godson) after the derailment of a Miami-to-Pittsburgh Amtrak train in which they were traveling.

The following Thanksgiving eve, Travolta was piloting the Gulfstream from Florida to Maine. Among his eight passengers were wife Kelly Preston and seven-month-old son Jett. While flying 39,000 feet at 600 miles an hour over Washington, D.C., the jet lost its electrical power. Travolta's "Mayday" alert reportedly led to the shutdown of Dulles and National airports and the Baltimore-Washington International airport. During his emergency landing, all four of the jet's tires burst. "Well," Travolta recalled three years later, "there are very few scenarios that could be worse, other than an actual crash."

During the ordeal, Travolta realized that he was in harm's way. But this near-tragedy in no way dampened his enthusiasm for being airborne. "For me," he declared in 1995, "outside of acting, which is my favorite thing to do, aviation is the juice that keeps me alive."

Twenty-Eight

"Without It, I Wouldn't Have Lived Longer Than John Belushi"

When he was making his screen debut in *The Devil's Rain*, Travolta was introduced to Scientology by Joan Prather, one of the actresses in the film. Since then, he has been a devotee of the Church of Scientology, founded by science fiction writer L. Ron Hubbard in the 1950s and described in its literature as "an applied religious philosophy." To its devotees, Scientology is a religion. But to others, it is a cult.

"L. Ron Hubbard discovered that your true potential lies in the mind that you use every day," explains another Scientology pamphlet. "He called it your *analytical* mind. Analytical because it analyzes information. . . . You can't seem to let go of the physical and emotional pain in your life, because it's locked up in the second part of the mind—the *reactive mind*. If the analytical mind is like a computer, then the reactive mind is like a computer virus that has infected it. . . . Without a reactive mind, you will think clearly, act rationally and be yourself again. This state is called Clear. Tens of thousands of people are Clears. You can be, too." The bible of Scientology is *Dianetics*, described as "the most popular and effective book on the human mind ever published."

Travolta is quoted in the literature: "Dianetics put me into the big time. I always had the ability to be somewhat successful, but Dianetics freed me up to the point where something really big could happen, without interference."

Other celebrities, including Tom Cruise, Kirstie Alley, Lisa Marie Presley, Anne Archer, Isaac Hayes, Chick Corea, and folk singer Melanie are Scientology members. Scientology critics have claimed that celebrities have been lured into the church. "One of my jobs was to get celebrities active, to convince them to hustle and promote Scientology," explained ex-Scientologist Robert Vaughn Young, in an article in the *Washington Post*. Richard N. Leiby, the author of the piece, continued, "Defectors from the church . . . contend Scientology is a destructive, money-oriented cult bent on world domination. . . . The church denies all such charges."

Whatever it is or isn't, Scientology certainly has worked for Travolta. Midway through the second season on *Welcome Back, Kotter*, a time when he was coping with the demands of instant fame, he declared, "Fortunately, I'm very much into Scientology. It's made my life simpler by helping me to understand the other person. This past year has been so fantastic that it could have made me go bonkers if Scientology hadn't kept me sane." At the zenith of his *Saturday Night Fever* fame, he declared, "I'd get very depressed for no reason. Psychoanalysis wasn't for me, but Scientology made sense to me right away because it seemed like a means of self-help." Marilu Henner, Travolta's friend and on-again-off-again lover, reported in her autobiography, "Johnny loved Scientology, and said it made a tremendous difference [in his life]." "Without it," Travolta told writer Martin Amis in 1994, "I wouldn't have lived longer than John Belushi." And he cited L. Ron Hubbard while accepting two prizes he won for *Get Shorty*: the Golden Globe Award and American Comedy Award. Upon hearing his name called for the Golden Globe, he declared, "There's a quote by a great man, L. Ron Hubbard, who says, 'No man can be happy without having a goal, and no man can be happy without his faith in the ability to achieve that goal.' And you tonight have given me the faith that I can achieve my goals, and I thank you." After winning the American Comedy Award, he thanked "my friend L. Ron Hubbard who taught me to not take life so seriously, and to also force yourself to laugh and you'll keep laughing."

Travolta's public acknowledgment of Scientology has extended beyond awards ceremonies. In 1985 he supported the efforts of Church of Scientology followers who picketed a courthouse in Portland, Oregon, where an ex-Scientologist had won a $39 million damage suit against the church. Travolta arrived in town and gave a press conference, where he declared, "I've been a Scientologist for ten years now. I've received counseling and I give counseling. I feel it's time to stand up

Travolta and his *Look Who's Talking* costar, Kirstie Alley. Both are devoted Scientologists.

for what I believe in, and I certainly believe in Scientology."

In 1993, the Church of Scientology opened a "Celebrity Center" in Los Angeles, at its Sunset Boulevard headquarters. Travolta was the main attraction at a black-tie party in honor of the event. He has reported that he attends four or five Scientology-related functions annually in Hollywood.

The following year, as *Pulp Fiction* was being released, Travolta credited Scientology with helping to sustain him during his long years when he could not buy a role in a decent film. "Being involved in Scientology, the techniques are very helpful in times of stress," he declared. "I'm one of those icons who survived the normal life expectancy [of a star]. I don't know if I would have made it without Scientology. That's been my best friend. . . ."

Twenty-Nine

Kelly Preston . . . and Jett

W
hen he proposed to Kelly Preston, in the Palace Hotel restaurant in Gstaad, Switzerland, as the clock struck twelve on New Year's Eve, 1991, Travolta presented his beloved with a six-carat diamond ring. His exact words were "Kelly, will you marry me?" Preston screamed with excitement, before accepting. Present were Jonathan D. Krane, Travolta's manager, and his wife, actress Sally Kellerman. Of Preston, Travolta's sister Ellen remarked, "She's a doll. Everyone in the family is thrilled." Added Krane, "Kelly will make him a wonderful wife. She understands him."

In 1995, Travolta described Preston to Liz Smith as "sort of a Grace Kelly type, well-spoken and beautiful, something like our mutual friend Holland Taylor—you know, sophisticated and glamorous. Kelly is a wonderful actress and she can even do character parts. She was in *Twins* with Arnold Schwarzenegger."

Travolta and Preston were married at midnight on September 5, 1991, at the Hotel de Crillon in Paris, by a French Scientology minister. They were in France for the premiere of *Eyes of an Angel* (which then was known as *The Tender*) at the Deauville Film Festival. "I'm literally high," was Travolta's response after being asked to by a reporter to describe his feelings.

Travolta and Preston became acquainted during the filming of *The Experts*, and their first encounter occurred when she screen-tested for the film. They began dating in Vancouver during the summer of 1990, when he was filming *Look Who's Talking Too* and she was shooting a thriller called *Run*.

Preston was born in Honolulu on October 13, 1963. Upon her parents' divorce, she lived in Australia for fourteen years before returning to Hawaii. She has recalled that, while in high school, she had a forewarning that she would come to know Travolta. Preston was in a moviehouse whose outside was adorned with a poster from *Grease*. While looking at the poster, she had a "feeling" that she would "be with

him forever." At the time, she did not even have an interest in pursuing an acting career.

Travolta and Preston, on the set of *The Experts*.

While in high school, Preston began working in a local advertising agency. "I really liked the ad business," she once remarked. "But I realized a lot of people [in the business] had ulcers. So I went into acting."

First she studied drama at USC and UCLA. While still an undergraduate, she landed a role on *Capitol*, a daytime soap. In 1983 she was a regular on the short-lived TV series *For Love and Honor*, an *Officer and a Gentleman* clone in which she played a general's daughter. Her other film credits include *Amazon Women on the Moon*, *Arthur Miller's The American Clock*, *Cheyenne Warrior*, *Christine*, *Double Cross*, *52 Pick-up*, *Love Is a Gun*, *Metalstorm: The Destruction of Jared Syn*, *Mischief*, *Only You*, *Secret Admirer*, *Spellbinder*, *A Tiger's Tale*, and, more recently, *Precious*, *Mrs. Munck*, *From Dusk Till Dawn*, and *Little Surprises*, an Oscar-nominat-

Preston (top right), along with (clockwise from bottom) Leaf Phoenix, Tate Donovan, Lea Thompson, Larry B. Scott and (center) Kate Capshaw, attending *SpaceCamp*.

ed short directed by Jeff Goldblum.

In 1985, Preston had married actor Kevin Gage, with whom she appeared in *SpaceCamp*, but the union ended in divorce two years later; she still was wed to Gage when she filmed *The Experts*. Travolta has acknowledged his attraction to her at that time, but did not pursue a relationship because of her unavailability.

After her divorce, Preston became involved with a pre-*ER* George Clooney. In April 1989, she became engaged to Charlie Sheen. *His* engagement ring was twenty-five carats and cost $200,000. "She's the first person who loves me and won't put up with my *bleep*," Sheen declared. But their betrothal lasted only through April 1990. Preston was unattached when she and Travolta hooked up in Vancouver several months later. In a November 4, 1990, *Parade* magazine profile of Preston, writer James Brady coyly noted, "Her new boyfriend is both an actor and a pilot."

"They, as a couple, seem to be nice," one observer noted at the 1995 Los Angeles Films Critics Association awards ceremony, where Travolta was honored as Best Actor for *Pulp Fiction*. "Sometimes you see [Hollywood] couples who seem to want to have absolutely nothing to do with each other. But this was not at all so [with Travolta and Preston]."

Seven months after their marriage, they became the parents of a son, whom they named Jett. Travolta, of course, has always loved children. Throughout his bachelorhood, he enjoyed the company of his fifteen nieces and nephews. "He's really a family guy," Amy Heckerling, his director in *Look Who's Talking* and *Look Who's Talking Too*, once observed.

Preston vamping Andrew McCarthy in *Only You.*

"You never see him without relatives and dogs." Indeed, his characters in *Look Who's Talking*, *Shout*, *Eyes of an Angel*, and *Chains of Gold* are almost autobiographical in that they share a deep feeling and concern for youngsters from infants to teens.

You can safely bet your set of *Grease* trading cards that, unlike so many movie star parents, Travolta is not an absentee father. "My son, he's just . . . he's *soooo* . . . I'm so in love with him," Travolta gushed to an interviewer when Jett was three years old. Later on, he added, "He's the most perfect child in regard to what he needs and wants. I mean, he's just so happy and complacent and understanding, but I think we also give him the space to be whoever he is."

Upon winning his Golden Globe for *Get Shorty*, Travolta thanked the makers of the film and his costars, managers, agents, and friends—everyone but his wife and child! Several minutes later, he told Dick Clark, who was interviewing winners backstage, "My wife Kelly and my son Jett mean more [to me] than my life. I didn't get a chance to thank them, and I'm glad I'm getting a chance to thank them now. Thank you, honey . . ." Several weeks later, he won an American Comedy Award for the same film. Again, he thanked his costars, director, writers, producers, "friends and family" . . . This time, he remembered Kelly before leaving the stage. "And my wife, my wife," he exclaimed. "I love her so much, and she showed a sense of humor by marrying me!"

Back in 1978, a full fifteen years before he was to become a father, Travolta declared, "The day I find out my wife is pregnant I'll be a maniac.

"Every time I have visions of being a father, I get shivers."

Thirty

Sex and the Single Travolta

I n his notorious and provocative 1983 interview in *Rolling Stone*, Travolta admitted that he had lost his virginity at age thirteen. But he wasn't naming names.

While filming *The Boy in the Plastic Bubble*, Travolta fell in love with his costar, Diana Hyland—and experienced the heart-break of her death. Travolta has stated that, had she lived, he and Hyland would have married.

Prior to his union with Kelly Preston, Travolta had over the years been linked with a number of women. In 1976, New York *Daily News* reporter George Maksian wrote, "He dates a girl named Julie, the younger sister of Marcia Strassman, who plays [Gabe] Kaplan's wife on [*Welcome Back, Kotter*]." Maksian asked Travolta about what attracts him to a woman. "I look for communication between the sexes; a sense of humor," the young actor responded. "I don't go for looks. Sure, it's nice to have, but I don't put total weight on it."

In 1980, gossip columnist Jack Martin reported that Travolta, who then was promoting *Urban Cowboy*, admitted having an affair with Olivia Newton-John while the two were filming *Grease*. Of his then costar, Debra Winger, he declared, "She's incredible. I picked her myself for the part in the movie, and *obviously* you pick someone you are attracted to." He also had a "very big thing" with Joan Prather, with whom he appeared in *The Devil's Rain*. (However, in 1980, Prather explained, "We were together for three months [during the filming of *The Devil's Rain*], but I wouldn't call it dating. We were just the very best of friends.") Later on, he also had "something of a romance" with Brooke Shields.

Around the time of the release of *Urban Cowboy*, it was reported that Travolta had dreamed about "making love to Jane Fonda." Allegedly, the actress, seventeen years Travolta's senior, reminded him of Diana Hyland. "I have this fantasy I'm making love to her. I get it often," Travolta was quoted in the *London Daily Mirror*. "Besides being very attractive and sexy . . . I think she's a very smart lady." He also told

Rolling Stone, "I think she's probably a wild woman in bed." Travolta already had met Fonda, who then was married to Tom Hayden. When queried if Fonda was aware of his fantasy, Travolta responded, "Oh, sure. I hear she told someone she was flattered."

Also in 1980, it was reported that Travolta had become obsessed with Catherine Deneuve. They had met while she and Gerard Depardieu were in New York to promote *The Last Metro*, a film they recently had made with François Truffaut. A rumor spread that Deneuve had been spotted in Philadelphia, where Travolta was filming *Blow Out*. The *New York Post*, beneath the headline TRAVOLTA IS DRIVEN CRAZY BY NEW LOVE CATHERINE DENEUVE, quoted Deneuve as gushing superlatives about Travolta. "He's the most exciting man I have ever met," she is reported to have said. "And I have never experienced such mental or physical exhilaration with anyone before!" Travolta's comments were equally panting: "I look at her and I simply die with each breath I take. She is a dream who simply floats through air. She doesn't walk, she actually glides like a soft white cloud drifting across the blue heaven."

Deneuve was reported to have been present during the filming of

Prior to his marriage, Travolta's most publicized romantic relationship was with Marilu Henner. They met while appearing in the road company of *Grease*.

Travolta and Olivia Newton-John, in *Two of a Kind*.

a sequence in which Travolta was speeding through the Philadelphia streets. At one point, he took a right turn and his vehicle, zipping along at seventy miles per hour, headed straight toward the city's Mummers Day Parade. Deneuve was quoted as having "sobbed." "When it was finished, I burst into tears and thanked God that John didn't hurt or kill himself."

A romance novelist could not have written more cornball dialogue. The fact of the matter was that Deneuve—after she and Depardieu attended the San Francisco Film Festival in conjunction with *The Last Metro*—simply had returned to France. The *New York Post* story was pure fabrication.

As a movie star/sexual icon, Travolta has been the subject of many such outlandish reports. In a 1985 interview, he even cited an unnamed, "fairly famous" woman "who said, 'Oh yeah, I've had sex with John.' I've never had anything with her. It's par for the course."

Easily Travolta's most public—and very much documented—romantic relationship was with Marilu Henner. The two met in 1972, when they were unknown young actors on the national tour of *Grease*. Chapter Six of Henner's 1994 autobiography *By All Means Keep on Moving* is titled "When Mari Met Johnny." "Johnny," of course, is Travolta. Henner chose to play on the movie title *When Harry Met Sally* because, as Billy Crystal's and Meg Ryan's fictional characters, she and Travolta were close, platonic friends before becoming lovers.

When they were cast in *Grease*, Travolta and Henner were under twenty-one, and the youngest members of the company. Their attraction was immediate, but both kept their curiosity in check because Travolta already had a girlfriend, Denise Wurms. She and he had grown up together. They had been dating since he was fourteen, and Henner respected the fact that Wurms was in the picture romantically. So she and Travolta became best friends.

Then Travolta and Wurms parted. Henner reported that her first sexual encounter with Travolta came in San Francisco, in a Travelodge near Fisherman's Wharf. The pair now were a definite hot item, with romance being as much a part of their involvement as sexual attraction. However, their relationship was fated to cool. One factor causing this was their ages. Feelings and desires aside, both simply were too young to consider making a lifetime commitment. Another was the pressure on Travolta as his career began to skyrocket.

Henner and Travolta were reunited professionally when both were cast in *Over Here!* Over the years, they were to enjoy a deep friendship, and on-again, off-again relationship. "I've been *that* close to marrying her," Travolta noted in 1980, "but every time we got ready to do it, I backed off. Perhaps in the end I will marry her." Five years later, he declared, "We're together when we're together. It's sad to say, but I don't know if marriage has the same significance anymore." Of course, Travolta and Henner never did wed.

They have maintained their friendship. Henner was, in fact, cast in two of Travolta's films: *Perfect*, in which she plays Sally, the health club-obsessed pal of Laraine Newman's Linda; and *Chains of Gold*, as Jackie, a lawyer and ex-girlfriend of Scott, Travolta's character.

Jackie has prostituted herself by becoming the attorney of Carlos the crack king. She and Scott meet after not having seen each other for several years. They go out to dinner and reminisce—and fact and fiction merge as Jackie recalls "that first time in San Francisco. You know, at the Travelodge."

Travolta has been romantically and sexually linked—real or imagined—to assorted actresses who have never been his costars. Among them: Brooke Shields *(above)*, Catherine Deneuve *(opposite)* and Jane Fonda.

Travolta receives a screen credit as cowriter of *Chains of Gold*. One can assume that this bit of dialogue was one of his contributions to the script.

Back in 1978, when he was in the *Saturday Night Fever* spotlight, Travolta declared, "Before I was famous, I had what you would call one-night experiences. But I find these are much more exciting in my fantasies than in reality."

Five years later, Travolta gave the *Rolling Stone* interview in which he discussed the loss of his virginity. He also revealed that, while not into one-night stands, he was far from monogamous. "To be really honest," he said, "I'd have to say I'm afraid to commit to one person, so I have maybe three or four people on the line." He declared that the "gypsylike" lifestyle of a professional actor allowed him to be in love with several women at once, adding, "I'm usually attracted to women who have big sexual appetites and fewer sexual hang-ups."

Travolta admitted a passion for women who were otherwise unavailable: "Now there are a few people I'd like to see who are tied up—like Lesley Ann Warren. She's very sexy." He declared that the first

girl he ever kissed was black. He was twelve. She was sixteen—and she also gave him his first taste of marijuana. He smoked reefer between the ages of sixteen and eighteen, and he tried cocaine around this time, but drugs never became avocations because he does not "have good physical reactions to them."

Travolta's then-disinterest in monogamy in no way indicates a lack of respect for women. Another 1983 article, this one in *Family Weekly* magazine, featured a byline by Travolta. It was titled WHAT I STILL DON'T UNDERSTAND ABOUT WOMEN, and was published the week of the opening of *Staying Alive*—and its content can be contrasted to the *Rolling Stone* revelations. In the piece, Travolta discussed his feelings about and attraction to women, and his theories on what makes for a successful relationship.

"I know that some women have perceived me as the macho guy in control, but that's not really the case," Travolta wrote. "I'm as vulnerable in a relationship as the woman is. I want to meet someone halfway." His sister Margaret was quoted as declaring that Travolta "regards women as people, not sex objects." Added sister Ann, "John totally adores and respects women. I think the independence and assertiveness that he saw in our mother and in us, his sisters, helped to give him the respect and admiration that he has for women today."

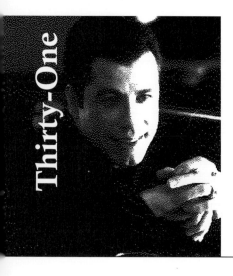

Thirty-One

Is He or Isn't He?–Who Cares!

Back in 1990, the *National Enquirer*, a tabloid newspaper never known for discretion, ran an article headlined I WAS JOHN TRAVOLTA'S GAY LOVER. In it, Paul Barresi, a former porn movie actor (in films both gay and straight) claimed that, in 1983, Travolta followed him "into a health club and arranged a date . . . while Barresi was stark naked in the shower!" Barresi, who had a small role in *Perfect*, claimed that he and Travolta carried on a two-year-long affair, at the same time the actor was dating Marilu Henner, Debra Winger, and Olivia Newton-John.

For publishing his story, the *Enquirer* paid Barresi $100,000.

Several months later, a remorseful Barresi told the gay magazine the *Advocate*, "I would like to apologize not only to John Travolta and his family but also to the gay community and anyone else I may have offended. I cashed in. If I could do it over again, I wouldn't. . . . I sold out one of the dearest, closest friends I ever had." While regreting that he had accepted money to exploit Travolta, Barresi did not state that he had lied about the relationship.

Throughout his career, Travolta has been hounded by rumors of his alleged gayness. And he deserves the final word on the subject. In the 1983 *Rolling Stone* piece, Nancy Collins asked him flat out if he were gay. His answer, in a word, was "No." In a 1985 exchange with Margy Rochlin in *Interview* magazine, he was asked if he minded being queried about his sexual preference. "Oh, that," he responded. "That's been asked of me before. If the answer is 'No,' then what is the big beef?" Rochlin's follow-up: "Why do you think people are so fascinated by your sex life?" Travolta's answer: "It has always been part of human nature to question that about people. It didn't strike me as a shocking question. It's been asked of other actors, stars, rock musicians, writers." He went on to add, "Sex is part of human nature, and I don't know why such a big deal is made out of it."

When queried on the subject a decade later, after he had married and become a parent, Travolta declared, "When I look at things like

Travolta as Tony Manero in *Staying Alive*. No matter Travolta's own sexual preferences, the tight clothing he wore onscreen would make him as appealing to gay men as to heterosexual women.

that, I look at the intent behind it. Is the intent to degrade, or destroy someone? If it's not, then you can have a decent conversation on the subject. But if it's actually an intent to hurt? Then it's like any other intention to hurt."

During his 1994 appearance on *Saturday Night Live*, Travolta good-naturedly lampooned the public's fascination with his sexuality. In one skit, he played Count Dracula, and two visitors to his castle (Janeane Garofalo, Kevin Nealon) speculate on whether the count is gay. "I'm a vampire," Dracula protests, as he goes about defending his heterosexuality. "I'm not gay. I suck human blood."

At one point, the count proclaims, "I am secure in my masculinity": a declaration that is double-edged, in that it also might have come from Travolta.

Thirty-Two

Travolta on Travolta

At an age when most of his contemporaries were attending college or starting their first jobs, with their career accomplishments years into the future, Travolta already had become a teen idol on *Welcome Back, Kotter* and a movie icon in *Saturday Night Fever*. During this period and beyond, he attempted to deal with the pressures of his sudden fame, reflect on his status within his profession, and keep his life in perspective while not ignoring dreams that had not yet been realized.

An actor has no privacy. That's part of the deal, and there's no point in griping about it. Nobody, after all, made me become an actor. And it's not that I was unaware of what Barbarino could do for me: I knew he had the potential to be a star-maker. But acting is where my heart is. If you told me I could have millions of dollars but only if I stopped acting, I wouldn't take the money. . . . I'd be lying, though, if I didn't admit that I wish I could have privacy when I wanted it.—*1977*

By the time I'm thirty I'd like to be established as a movie star. But it's so hard to predict.—*1977*

My life and career have been a fairy tale. But my father taught me to have a high integrity about work. If my career ever went down the drain, I would not be too proud to work in the supermarket where I started.—*1977*

My fans will have to grow with me. I don't want to be considered a teen idol the rest of my life.—*1978*

When I first saw my name up on a billboard, I felt it was really glamorous. But then I remembered the Travolta Tire Exchange sign my father had in New Jersey.—*1979*

Nah—I'm not a prisoner of my fame. I love it! But, of course, I enjoy even more the respect I get as an actor. I wouldn't like to deal with just the fame itself.—*1980*

It's like we're the last of a breed. Don't get me wrong. I'm not forgetting Redford or Newman or Pacino or De Niro or Dustin Hoffman. But those guys are of a different generation. I'm talking about ten years from now. Who'll be the sexy stars ten years from now? Me, Richard Gere, Stallone. That's it.—*1983*

Regarding the above quote:

Oh boy, did I get in trouble for that one . . . It was actually quoted to me by a studio head. I thought when I said it I had explained it in context. Like, "It appears to be . . ." or "According to . . ." And the way it was edited . . . I mean, who knows? Every year there is a whole new crop of people.—*1985*

Life is so much better now. I still have my place in Santa Barbara which keeps me sane and out of the rat race. I have gotten more comfortable with who and what I am. You know all that attention coming at you at once, it's overwhelming. But I decided you either love it or leave it and I decided to love it and stay with it.—*1984*

In 1989, when his career was at one of several nadirs, Travolta granted an interview to journalist Pat Broeske—reportedly the first major one he had given since 1985. In it, he discussed the manner in which he dealt with his tumble from the top of celluloid stardom.

> How about if people don't go crazy for me, but they just like me. And they come to see my movies. . . . The weird thing is, I thought *Saturday Night Fever* was just going to be a stepping-stone . . .

> That was the first time I heard the words, "Your career is over."—regarding the opening of *Moment by Moment*.

> Whatever you do, you shouldn't depict me as a victim. Because if you depict me as one, you'll be wrong. I don't feel like a victim. I don't play violins for myself. I never have.

> It doesn't matter what people think about me. They can say what they want. But the fact is, they've never been where I've been.

> I was feeling sort of out of it. Then two wonderful things happened. Whoopi Goldberg wanted to make a movie with me—and she was the hottest thing going. And Princess Di wanted to dance with me. And I thought, even when things are bad for me, they're pretty damn good.—describing his period after *Perfect*.

As he aged, Travolta has mellowed, and become more reflective of his early success.

> I had this need for success young. I didn't have the

With Kelly Preston in *The Experts*.

patience to wait. If I'd gone fifteen years and never quite made it, maybe I'd have said, "It's not in the cards for me, so I'll go back and do summer theater." At least I know there's an audience that does want to see me.—1990

It's funny, one movie can make you, and one movie can remake you. It's like I went to the moon, then came back down to earth, and now I get to go to Mars or some place.—at the time of the release of *Pulp Fiction*, 1994

I mean, technically, I didn't *go* anywhere to come back from, and you know, [the critics] were writing the same thing about *Look Who's Talking*. What I realized is that there's a group of people, who, when they didn't get to see the kind of work on the kind of level that they expected, then to them I was gone.—1995

Whether you're Sean Connery, Paul [Newman] or Warren [Beatty] or Dustin [Hoffman], your best times, your most interesting roles are after forty. Let's face it, you have to live life to contribute to stage, screen, or books.—1994

Thirty-Three

Others on Travolta

His Career

For Travolta, it's a triumphant starring debut. In a less engaging actor's hands, Tony [Manero] could have been insufferably arrogant and dense. But Travolta's big slab of a face is surprisingly expressive, revealing a little boy's embarrassment and hurt as well as a stud's posturing. Travolta understands Tony with his whole body—needless to say, he can dance up a storm—and you can't keep your eyes off him. It's a fresh, funny, downright friendly performance.

—DAVID ANSEN, REVIEWING *SATURDAY NIGHT FEVER* IN *NEWSWEEK*, 1977

[His career] will be a formidable one. It's on its way already and the boy will be a superstar.

—HAROLD J. KENNEDY, WHO DIRECTED TRAVOLTA IN THE SUMMER THEATER PRODUCTION OF *BUS STOP*, 1978

Today Travolta is the biggest star in the world, bar none. Just the mere fact that he's in a project, or might be in it, turns it into a major event.

—MICHAEL EISNER, PRESIDENT OF PARAMOUNT PICTURES, 1978

For John to be able to [become a movie star] means there's hope for everybody. I envy John Travolta the actor; but I don't envy John Travolta the person. He's so sweet and totally untouched by the whole situation.

—RON PALILLO, *WELCOME BACK, KOTTER* COSTAR, 1978

John is paving the way for a lot of young TV actors who are very talented. And I'm next.

—ROBERT HEGYES, *WELCOME BACK, KOTTER* COSTAR, 1978

With Sid Caesar in *Grease*.

. . . Travolta does give an exceptionally convincing performance, a seamless blend of cockiness and vulnerability. What remains to be seen is whether it is really acting, or merely typecasting.

—JOHN SIMON, REVIEWING *SATURDAY NIGHT FEVER*
IN *REVERSE ANGLE*, 1978

John, he's got plenty to learn, but he will. And *then* he'll use it correctly. When I saw [*Urban*] *Cowboy*, I said, "The kid's got it all."

—JAMES CAGNEY, 1980

He had a vision of where he wanted to be. I have a crazy theory. I think John created a vacuum and then stepped into it. He *willed* his success.

—TOM MOORE, WHO EARLIER HAD DIRECTED
TRAVOLTA ON STAGE IN *GREASE*, 1980

The magic ingredient in the meteoric rise of John Travolta is that every teenage boy wants to be like him and every teenage girl falls in love with him.

—*THE HOLLYWOOD REPORTER STAR PROFILES*, 1984

I've just cast a pretty big film. I think the name of every actor in the business between the ages of twenty-two and

Dancing with Finola Hughes in
Staying Alive.

thirty-five came up. And I never heard a single mention of John. He doesn't even make the casting list these days.

—UNIDENTIFIED MOVIE EXECUTIVE, QUOTED BY PAT BROESKE, 1989

I have this theory that people are embarrassed about anything they liked in the seventies. I think people hold their hatred for discos against John. And for bell-bottoms. And the rest of the fads. But the fact is, John's not responsible for what we did during that decade.

—AMY HECKERLING, DIRECTOR OF *LOOK WHO'S TALKING* AND *LOOK WHO'S TALKING TOO*, 1989

He'll have to have a moderate hit so he can be viable for the big pictures, and compete with the Kevin Costners. Don't think it can't be done, dear. Show business has no memory.

—LOIS ZETTER, TRAVOLTA'S FORMER AGENT, 1989

You know what I'd like? I'd like to do the second

Saturday Night Fever sequel. I'd bring John's character to Hollywood and have his story parallel what's happened to John. But—we would have a happy ending.

—James Bridges, director of *Urban Cowboy* and *Perfect*, 1989

People said, "John Travolta, you're kidding, you can get any actor in the world." We [Bender and Tarantino] said John was the bottom line. People didn't understand why we didn't want to use a superstar. But John was the guy Quentin wanted.

—Lawrence Bender, producer of *Pulp Fiction*, 1994

It drove me crazy in the last five years seeing John in the movies he's been in. I looked at them and said, "Why aren't directors taking advantage of him?" Don't they know they have this great natural resource out there?

—Quentin Tarantino, 1994

[Travolta's] long-haired, earringed Vincent Vega is one smart-ass thug, and the fans and reporters can't get enough of his new incarnation.

—Howard Feinstein, reporting from the
Cannes Film Festival, 1994

If anyone holds this movie together, it isn't Tarantino—it's John Travolta. He strolls through it without a wink of vanity, having long since relinquished the oily posing of *Saturday Night Fever* in favor of the first law of cool: Don't try to be cool. The very title, *Pulp Fiction*, sounds like a description of his face—luscious but squashy, easily bruised, the look of a former pretty boy who can still inspire tall tales. While Tarantino clamors for our attention, Travolta knows that he has it and isn't going to lose it in a hurry. He can afford to rumple and fatten his

With Lily Tomlin in *Moment by Moment.*

character, turning Vince into a slob and a patsy . . . Travolta has the nerve, in the midst of what feels like an action movie, to remind us of the pleasures of inactivity, the deep need to hang out.

—ANTHONY LANE, REVIEWING *PULP FICTION* IN *THE NEW YORKER*, 1994

. . . Travolta [puts] on a dazzling demonstration of what being a movie star is all about . . . to answer the big question first, he's never been better. . . . Travolta looks great, gets to be cooler than everyone else at all times, and delivers a performance of enormous subtlety and charm that also manages to be broadly appealing.

—TODD MCCARTHY, REVIEWING *GET SHORTY* IN *VARIETY*, 1995

His Personality

He is polite, soft-spoken, even a little shy.

—ALICE KOENIGSBERG, WRITING IN *US* MAGAZINE, 1978

The public Travolta, personable and shy, canny and eager, is like a picture of a child's coloring book, where only the bold, broad outlines of a figure are provided.

The drawing will take any colors you want. Only the original artist holds the full, definitive master sketch, which he shares sparingly.

—*TIME*, 1978

John is the most sensitive person I know, male or female.

—JERRY WURMS, HIGH SCHOOL FRIEND, 1980

I've worked with a lot of big stars, and he's the only one who's ever actually knocked on my trailer door just to come in and talk and hang out.

—CHRISTIAN SLATER, COSTAR OF *BROKEN ARROW*, 1995

For years, he couldn't get arrested. This [*Pulp Fiction*] came, and he was loving it. But he couldn't quite relax. Yet he was very nice, very sweet and solicitous and very pleasant when you spoke to him. But extremely uptight.

—AN OBSERVER, AT THE LOS ANGELES FILM CRITICS ASSOCIATION AWARDS CEREMONY, 1995

John Travolta embodies cool.

—RENÉ RUSSO, COSTAR OF *GET SHORTY*, 1995

After the devastating reviews of *Moment by Moment* in 1978, Travolta hastily retreated from the public eye, reevaluating the manner in which he related to those whose loyalty was not a given. Some members of the press were not amused.

I personally observed during the location filming of [*Urban*] *Cowboy* that the schizoid Travolta is shy or arrogant, cooperative or recalcitrant, generous or selfish, trusting or paranoid depending on the circumstances. Travolta is a prince around people who massage his fragile ego with flattery and adulation. But with strangers or people who have failed to demonstrate their loyalty, the insecure Travolta erects formidable barriers to protect himself.

—MIKE GRECO, WRITING IN *AFTER DARK*, 1980

[He has become] as reclusive as Garbo and as difficult at times as Sinatra.

—*LIFE* MAGAZINE, 1980

Other Travolta observers were more thoughtful in their commentary.

He is at one moment a kid with a passion for acting, airplanes, and Scientology, at another a man grappling with the pressures of sudden wealth, power, and celebrity, and at heart a serious actor just beginning to learn his most demanding role: John Travolta, superstar.

—*NEWSWEEK*, 1980

Still more were—and are—won over by him.

I always go to these big-star interviews hoping I won't be disappointed in whatever wild egomania or paranoia or whatever is about to be exposed. Travolta was a completely delightful surprise. His fans are right to love him and I'm one of them.

—LIZ SMITH, 1980

For two decades, on and off, I have been interviewing famous people. And I have to confess that I have never interviewed anyone as generous as John Travolta: generous with his time, his trouble, his attentiveness.

—MARTIN AMIS, WRITING IN *THE NEW YORKER*, 1995

But as anyone who's been around John for more than

five minutes will tell you, there isn't a nicer human being in Hollywood. He's a better person than he is a player. And in that sense, he's the same friendly, charming guy I met in the seventies.

—Judson Klinger, writing in *Playboy*, 1996

Not only is Travolta a man who will share his very chocolate soufflé with you, he's also constitutionally gener-ous—in his attentiveness, in his honest curiosity as to what the heck the person in front of him might be all about, in his boyish charm—which seems to be no act. . . . The mannish boy endures in the eternally boyish man."

—Fred Schruers, writing in *Rolling Stone*, 1996

His Celebrity

Travolta has been described as having a playful sense of humor. "He's a terminally silly person and nobody ever knows it," observed Marcia Strassman, his *Welcome Back, Kotter* costar. He also is an excellent mimic, with his impersonations transcending sexual and racial boundaries. He has been known to entertainingly copy, among others, Elvis Presley, Stevie Wonder, Warren Beatty, Cyndi Lauper, James Stewart—and his father smoking a cigar.

Travolta's fans were allowed a glimpse of their hero's talent for mimicry in 1994, when he guest hosted *Saturday Night Live*. He appeared in skits in which he hilariously impersonated Barbra Streisand (garbed in a circa 1964 sailor suit, and being interviewed on *Coffee Talk*

With Linda Richman), Marlon Brando (being interviewed by Larry King), and Boris Karloff playing Count Dracula.

And when it comes to his own celebrity, he has no trouble being John Travolta.

> In terms of lifestyle John's very much a movie star in the old tradition. He loves being a movie star, and he makes no bones about it.
>
> —Jamie Lee Curtis, costar of *Perfect*, 1985

> There's an innate sense of glamour about John. He lives his life in a way that's exciting to hear about.
>
> —James Bridges, director of *Urban Cowboy* and *Perfect*, 1985

> John taught me about the roller-coaster ride of celebrity. You're only as good as your last movie. He said he figured out what was important to him—what he liked doing and how he wanted to live—instead of trying to get others' approval.
>
> —Kirstie Alley, costar of *Look Who's Talking*, 1990

> John has a self-confidence about himself. I don't think he feels any differently about himself now than he did during the *Perfect* and *Look Who's Talking* days. He loves being a movie star, but not in a "I need a bigger camper" way. He just loves it in a good way.
>
> —Barry Sonnenfeld, director of *Get Shorty*, 1995

> For me, [meeting Travolta] was like stepping into a Warhol poster—a Mao, an Elvis. It was like bumping into James Dean or Jimi Hendrix. You feel that John Travolta is so iconic that he ought to be dead. And he isn't; not anymore.
>
> —Martin Amis, writing in *The New Yorker*, 1995

Sources

The following sources were consulted during the preparation of this book.

Books

Henner, Marilu, with Jim Jerome. *By All Means Keep on Moving*. New York: Pocket Books, 1994.

Kennedy, Harold J. *No Pickle, No Performance: An Irreverent Theatrical Excursion from Tallulah to Travolta*. Garden City, New York: Doubleday & Company, 1978.

Reed, Rex. *Travolta to Keaton*. New York: William Morrow and Company, 1979.

Sackett, Susan. *The Hollywood Reporter Book of Box Office Hits*. New York: Billboard Books, 1990.

Simon, John. *Reverse Angle*. New York: Clarkson N. Potter, 1982.

Travolta, John. *Staying Fit!*. New York: Simon and Schuster, 1984.

Wanamaker, Marc, general editor. *The Hollywood Reporter Star Profiles*. New York: Gallery Books, 1984.

Webb, Michael, editor, *Hollywood: Legend and Reality*. Boston: Little Brown and Company, 1986.

Magazines and Newspapers

The Advocate; After Dark; Attenzione; Billboard; Brooklyn; Chicago Tribune; Christian Science Monitor; Dance Magazine; Family Weekly; Film Comment; Grooves; Interview; Life Magazine; Los Angeles Times; New York Daily News; New York; New York Newsday; New York Post; New York Times; The New Yorker; Newark Star-Ledger; Newsweek; The Observer (London); Parade Magazine; People; Photoplay; Playbill; Playboy; Rolling Stone; Seventeen; SoHo Weekly News; Teen Beat; Teen Pin-Ups; Teen Talk; Tiger Beat; Time; TV Guide; TV Stars Today; TV Superstar; US Magazine; Variety; Village Voice; Washington Post; Women's Wear Daily.

Index

Author Biographies

Rob Edelman is the author of *Great Baseball Films* (Citadel Press) and coauthor of *Angela Lansbury: A Life on Stage and Screen* (Birch Lane Press). He is contributing editor of *Leonard Maltin's Movie and Video Guide,* and his work appears in several other books (including *A Political Companion to American Film, The International Dictionary of Films and Filmmakers,* and *Leonard Maltin's Movie Encyclopedia*). He is the director of programming of Home Film Festival, which rents select videotapes by mail throughout the country, and he has written for dozens of periodicals (from *American Film* through the *Washington Post*).

Audrey E. Kupferberg is a film consultant, archivist, and appraiser. She is the former director of the Yale Film Study Center; assistant director of the National Center for Film and Video Preservation at the American Film Institute; and project director of the American Film Institute catalog. She is the coauthor of *Angela Lansbury: A Life on Stage and Screen.* She and Rob Edelman are married, and live in upstate New York.